Your
MAGNETIC
HEART

www.ruedigerschache.com
www.facebook.com/ruedigerschache

Project Credits

Cover Design: Brian Dittmar Design, Inc.   Special Sales Manager: Judy Hardin
Book Production: John McKercher   Rights Coordinator: Candace Groskreutz
Illustrator: Dana Sitarzewski   Publisher's Assistant: Bronwyn Emery
Translator: Emily Banwell   Customer Service Manager:
Copy Editor: Leah Lowthorp, Jessa Hurley   Christina Sverdrup
Managing Editor: Alexandra Mummery   Order Fulfillment: Washul Lakdhon
Editorial Intern: Jordan Collins   Administrator: Theresa Nelson
Acquisitions Intern: Sally Castillo   IT Support: Peter Eichelberger
Publicity Coordinator: Martha Scarpati   Publisher: Kiran S. Rana

Ordering
For bulk orders please contact:
Turner Publishing Company
4507 Charlotte Avenue, Suite 100
Nashville, TN 37209
Phone: (615) 255-2665
E-mail: orders@turnerpublishing.com

Your MAGNETIC HEART

*10 Secrets of Love,
Attraction and Fulfillment*

RUEDIGER SCHACHE

Library of Congress Cataloging-in-Publication Data
Schache, Ruediger.
[Geheimnis des Herzmagneten. English]
Your magnetic heart : 10 secrets of attraction, love and fulfillment /
Ruediger Schache.—U.S. ed.
p. cm.
ISBN 978-0-89793-637-8 (cloth) — ISBN 978-1-68442-491-7 (pbk.)
ISBN 978-0-89793-639-2 (ebook)
1. Animal magnetism.   2. Charisma (Personality trait)   3. Interpersonal attraction.
I. Title.
BF1156.P4S33 2013
158.2 — dc23   2012041683

Printed in the United States of America

Contents

"God doesn't play dice."

Albert Einstein
Physicist and philosopher
1879–1955

Preface

The things that happen between people are no coincidence. What has happened so far in your life was no coincidence. The kinds of relationships you have and how they unfold are no coincidence.

There is a power within you. It is the reason for everything that happens to you, and for every event that has shaped your life. It is the reason why particular people, and not others, have shown up in your life, and it even explains their actions. This power is constantly working, whether or not you believe in it and whether or not you want it to.

This power is the secret of your magnetic heart, and you have the ability to change it. In becoming more aware of this power, you will feel more and more love—for yourself, for your life, and for others. And the more clearly you feel this love in yourself, the more frequently you'll be able to attract loving people and experience fulfilling events.

If you open yourself up to the secrets of your magnetic heart, you will find that the things you desire come to you more easily.

The First Secret

"Every person who
wants to be close to you
is attracted by something
within your magnet.

Attraction

Why are some people practically drowning in affection, while others have to fight to find love?

Why are you attracted to a certain type of man or woman even though he or she might not be the best match for you?

Why do your relationships always seem to follow similar patterns, regardless of your efforts to change them?

Why can't your partner ever act any differently, no matter how hard he or she tries?

Why is it that, even when you wish for something with all your might, the universe gives you just the opposite—or nothing at all?

All of these situations happen because of a force exerted by your magnetic heart. This force operates in you regardless of your appearance, education, age, language, or status. On the one hand, this force is like a magnet—attracting certain people or circumstances to you or repelling them, and determining how you respond to a situation or are unaffected by it. At the same time, it's also a little like a computer program that guides you to behave in certain ways.

Everything Responds to Everything

You are much more than the physical matter you see around you. Your body, your thoughts, and your feelings are forms of energy that affect other energy forms. One result of this is that the principles of vibration and resonance, as exhibited by your magnetic heart, cause similar types—as well as opposites—to have particularly strong responses to each other. Because they "resonate" strongly with each other, however your interactions play out, you'll be able to sense if they feel right or wrong, pleasant or unpleasant. In turn, you'll respond consciously or subconsciously to these feelings with corresponding thoughts and actions.

Everything Happens for a Reason

My study and contemplation of the subject has shown me that, for every person who comes into your life and affects you emotionally in some way, 80 percent of the attraction comes from your magnetic heart and 20 percent comes from external factors. Even if certain people or events in your life seem to be unrelated, there is a connection—it's just not always apparent. The better you understand the secrets of your magnetic heart, the clearer the underlying purpose for such experiences will become, and you will embark on a wonderful journey of discovery about yourself and others.

Everything Has Meaning

Think about your last relationship or take a look at the person you are in a relationship with right now. Feelings of affection or love are not the only reason that you found each other. This person has (or had) something that you long for or that embodies something familiar or

3

similar to you. Most likely it is a combination of the two. Additionally, he or she has certain characteristics that are so different from your own that they will always cause some kind of conflict.

Regardless of what you experience together, there is a deeper purpose for your connection—in some way, the other person helps you find answers to two of life's most fundamental questions: "Who am I?" and "What is love?"

Through this connection, and through your exchanges and everyday interactions with this person, you learn much more about yourself than you would have ever learned alone. You either begin to love yourself and your life because this person is encouraging and nurtures your inner beauty, or his or her behavior keeps you in check and ultimately helps you find your strengths, self-confidence, and inner freedom. Sometimes this happens quickly and sometimes it takes a while, but it always has some significance.

Every interaction with another person has a purpose:
- *to reinforce your existing qualities*
- *to supplement something that may be missing in your life*
- *to help you grow in new ways*
- *to help you better understand yourself*

"The beginning is the most important part of any work."

Plato
Greek philosopher and scholar
427–347 BC

What Makes Up Your Magnetic Heart?
Do you like to go to the movies? Do you love novels or good stories? Why?

In addition to movies and stories being social and recreational experiences, they offer us an emotional experience. The people sitting in the theater during a romantic comedy are usually very different from those watching an action film. A documentary will usually have a very different audience than a fairy tale or fantasy film. Every movie attracts a certain audience because moviegoers are looking for a certain emotional experience.

Your magnetic heart is mostly made up of your personal, emotionally charged "film clips." All of the things you have experienced, or want to experience, make up your personal "emotional movie the-

5

ater." On some level, the people around you pick up on your clips and feel either attracted, ambivalent, or repelled—depending on the emotions that they, too, want to experience or avoid.

Understanding these basics can be the start of a fundamental change in your relationships. It can save you a lot of time you may otherwise spend searching for—and trying out—certain connections, while sparing you a good deal of disappointment. And if something doesn't turn out the way you had hoped, you'll spend less energy blaming yourself and more time focusing on your new direction. Knowing what your own heart magnet holds will allow you to consciously decide who you attract and you will become someone who is constantly learning about what makes other people act the way they do.

What and how you feel shapes what you project outwardly, and attracts people who are looking for just that— no matter what the reason.

Who You Attract and Why

You don't automatically attract people who best complement you; instead, you attract those who need what you are projecting. Below are some of the main attributes of your magnet, which can attract or repel others:

◆ your good and bad experiences, along with other people's experiences that you might have absorbed without realizing it

◆ your expectations, reflections, and fears, as well as those of other people
◆ your desires, ideas, goals, and internal decisions
◆ the true core of your being
◆ …and a few other influences that you will learn about later

The most powerful effects often come from components of your magnet that are the least obvious to you. If the true core of your being could determine what you project outwardly, you'd easily be able to attract the kinds of people and situations that best fit your life. You would be constantly amazed and overjoyed. It might feel as if things were happening magically because the events were resonating so closely with your deepest desires. One of the greatest gifts you can give yourself is to learn how to distinguish your innermost wants and needs from all the other influences and options.

The Masculine and Feminine Magnet
Knowing the difference between what men and women project is especially valuable when it comes to deciding what you are looking for in a partner and a relationship.

Every man has feminine aspects, and every woman has masculine qualities. Some characteristics that are commonly considered more feminine are: emotions, diplomacy, caring, empathy, social interests, interpersonal skills, and integration. The more masculine qualities include: reason, logic, dominance, action, exerting power, pursuing goals, and making decisions.

Men and women are subconsciously always looking to become part of "a whole." In other words, they are seeking the aspects that they are missing within themselves.

For most people, the internal masculine to feminine ratio (for men, or feminine to masculine for women) is somewhere between 60/40 and 70/30. It isn't important whether a man or a woman appears especially masculine or feminine at first glance. The person's type—the result of the characteristics that he or she demonstrates—exerts a much stronger attraction.

The levels of masculine and feminine energy within your magnet will determine how masculine or feminine the partners you attract will be.

The "Strong Woman–Weak Man" Paradox

Many independent women experience a strange phenomenon with the men they encounter: Men admire and respect them, but at the same time seem to be inexplicably afraid of them and are skittish of forming a close relationship.

This is because men are, on the one hand, attracted to the qualities that they may lack; on the other hand, they also want to feel "masculine" next to a woman. The more the woman exercises her masculine qualities in the relationship, the less her partner is able to do so. At the same time, such women long for emotional qualities in their male partners, but often don't consider them "real men" if they are *too* sensitive.

Let's look at another scenario: If a man is sensitive, willing to compromise, diplomatic, caring, and interested in the well-being of others, his magnet will project these feminine qualities. As a result, he will be attractive to women who may have many traditionally "masculine" qualities. These might include women who "hold their own" in the work arena and women who navigate the world by thinking about it rationally and solve problems through definitive action.

It is not what you do, say, or wear that is the key to the masculine or feminine qualities of your heart magnet— it is how you feel that counts.

If a man feels masculine (powerful, clear, self-confident, etc.), women will pick up on this and react much more strongly to it than they would to bodybuilding, masculine clothing, or status symbols.

Mark and His Muscles

Mark is an attractive, emotionally intelligent man with an open heart. He's interested in other people and is full of compassion. However, by his mid-thirties he had never been in a relationship where a woman wanted to live with him.

When breaking up, one of his girlfriends once told him that he was just missing a "certain something" that women found attractive. She could only describe it as a "masculine aura."

Mark was not the type to take defeat lying down. He repeatedly looked at himself in the mirror and thought about what he could do to become more masculine. Finally, he joined a gym and started working out several times a week. After more than a year, his body was in great shape, but there still wasn't a promising relationship in sight. Despite the intensive work on his appearance, Mark didn't feel like his situation had changed. He realized that his approach wasn't working. What shaped his aura were his feelings about himself—and he still felt inferior when it came to attracting women.

Mark looked for any hidden thoughts that could be programming his heart magnet with the message that he wasn't a complete man. He remembered seeing his father as a short-tempered, insensitive man who was incapable of showing his own wife respect and love. As a boy, Mark had decided never to treat women that way. If his father's behavior demonstrated what it meant to be a grown man, Mark didn't want to be one. In his efforts to be understanding, loving, and compassionate, Mark had kept himself from feeling and projecting his own masculine strengths. As a result, the women he met couldn't see those qualities either. They liked him as a friend and confidante, but rejected him as a man and a partner.

Mark realized that it was his choice: He could keep trying to be the opposite of his father, or he could yield to his deep longing for a life partner. Clearly, for him, the two things were incompatible. He decided to embrace his masculine qualities and allow them to be projected by his magnetic heart. He found it particularly helpful to silently reassure himself of his manliness in situations where he previously tried too hard to prove he was sensitive and considerate so that women would like him. Once he began doing this, Mark found that women became more interested in him—without any additional effort on his part. Finally allowing himself to feel his masculine side, in combination with his physically fit body, made him an attractive catch.

The Internal Switch:
How to Change Your Magnet's Projection Immediately
Imagine that you have an internal on–off switch. Can you see the switch in your mind's eye? Good! Its current position stands for whatever you are projecting right now.

What do you want to project outwardly from now on? For instance, if you are a female, do you want your partner to see you as an attractive woman? It's easy: Just start feeling like one! Imagine changing your internal switch to the setting "attractive, mature woman," or to "seductive femininity." Choose a concept that makes you say, "Yes, that's what I want!"—and then simply flip the switch and notice what happens to you.

With every step and every movement, realize that you are an attractive woman. You don't need to look in the mirror to talk yourself into it—just feel the change in yourself. Don't tell anyone else about it. Simply observe how people around you respond.

It isn't about what
your body looks like.
It is much simpler.
It's about what you are projecting!

Once you have created the right switch for yourself, things will probably start to change without your needing to do anything else. Your only job is to remain aware of your switch and feel what happens when you activate it.

You can use it to change any projection you want: from "victim" to "empowered person," "childish" to "mature," "shy" to "confident," or "needy" to "free." The switch is kind of a game, but it's also a very effective tool. It doesn't just solve a problem with a single person or situation, it does something much more fundamental. You will find that the change in your self-perception also affects other people and alters how they act toward you.

Don't Just Believe Blindly, See for Yourself!
The successful outcome of your projection doesn't depend upon your knowledge. It comes from observation and experience, and from how you feel about the nature of your reality. Knowledge gained through your perception and personal experience has a much stronger effect than information learned from a book. It becomes part of your being and gives you strength, security, and confidence. The more you realize how your life "works," the better protected you are from outside influences, and the stronger your heart magnet works to attract the things that belong with you.

Observe people—yourself and others. There is no better way to build confidence. Take your knowledge about the secret of your magnetic heart out into the world and see what transpires. Your perspective will never be the same again.

Watch couples and try to see how they complement each other. For instance, look at men who seem especially masculine. What kind of woman do you see with a macho man? In most cases, it will be a woman who embodies a great deal of femininity, even if that is based solely on her appearance. On this level alone, both parties could be very satisfied with the relationship. A very feminine woman attracts a great deal of masculine energy from a very "manly" man. The relationship clearly supports her sense of femininity, because whenever she looks at the man by her side she notices how different he is from her as a woman, thereby reinforcing her own femininity.

If a woman exhibits a range of masculine qualities, for instance because she was raised that way or because her job requires it, a noticeably masculine man could help her feel more feminine. Similarly, a very feminine partner can help a gentler man develop his masculine side.

If their respective heart magnets are working (usually subconsciously), men with feminine qualities tend to find women who have a similar level of masculine qualities. Looking at the couples around you will confirm this.

Using the secret of your magnetic heart will open up the path for you to work consciously on changing your projection, thus attracting the kind of partners who will support you in your inherent masculinity or femininity.

If you are a man hoping that your magnet will attract more feminine women than it has in the past, the goal is to increase your masculine presence—your self-confidence and your "way of being present." If you are a woman who wants to attract more masculine men,

14

develop a more feminine presence, one that includes your womanly qualities.

*If you want to change what
you are projecting, do less, feel more.
In particular, get in touch with yourself
and your wonderful being.*

Many women are looking for a father figure in their partners, and plenty of men are seeking a companion to act as a mother. Unless they are aware of this, people are subject to other's automatic responses to their magnets.

Once you realize what your magnet has done so far and what you actually want to experience, you can decide to "flip the switch." Clarity does not mean making decisions without any compromise. It simply means knowing what you really want to experience and feel—what is currently inside your magnet and what it is attracting. Clarity means knowing who you are, what you want, and how to make it happen.

Anna, Robert, and the Issue of Having Children

Ever since Anna, a thirty-two-year-old athletic trainer, could remember she had wanted children. One day she met Robert, a successful businessman who had similar family goals. They found each other attractive right away and got along very well. After two years, they moved in together and talked frequently about their shared plans for the future.

Soon, however, they started experiencing more and more tension, which didn't go away even after repeated discussion. The primary issue was that Robert was taking advantage of his much stronger financial position and demanding that Anna fulfill his image of how a partner should act. Above all, he wanted her to learn how to cook, iron his shirts, and keep the house tidy, even though he had found other ways to take care of those things before they moved in together. No matter what Anna did, her partner constantly made her feel like she was worth less than he was, and that she was less emotionally mature. She often felt she was being treated like a child.

One day, while thinking about her professional future, Anna asked a friend for advice. She was trying to decide what to do after leaving her job. The two friends brainstormed about situations where Anna had always felt good; after all, things that make your heart leap and your eyes shine usually indicate the right path. As they listed Anna's talents and skills, she realized that she blossomed around children, and that kids in turn particularly enjoyed her presence. As they talked *further, Anna realized she probably got along so well with children because she connected with them on their level—and suddenly she realized why her partner had been treating her like a child rather than an equal. It was because, on some level, she felt more comfortable in the role of a child than that of a grown woman. Robert was unconsciously responding to the feelings being projected by her heart magnet. For years he had delayed starting a family with her, making tired excuses, even though that had been his lifelong dream. Now Anna realized why. In a sense, Robert already had a child—her!*

Anna was deeply shaken by this discovery. She realized that her partner was just reacting to her own longing to feel like a child. Robert couldn't help but treat her in a "paternalistic" way because that's exactly what she was projecting.

But did that mean Anna should give up her desire to work with children? Did she need to abandon her childlike qualities if she wanted to build an adult relationship with her partner?

Anna learned about the secret of her magnetic heart and decided to try an experiment. She imagined an internal switch that she could change from "child" to "woman." Whenever she came home from work, she paused for a second and internally flipped the switch. She reminded herself that she was not a child, but rather an adult woman returning home to her adult partner.

She didn't tell Robert about her discovery—she simply observed what it was like to enter as a grown woman. On the very first evening of her experiment, she noticed that her partner started treating her more respectfully. Within a short period of time, their relationship changed dramatically. The more often Anna reminded herself to feel like a woman, the more Robert treated her as an equal partner. His desire to have children with her returned, and his demands for her to perform housework stopped completely. Together, they started to look for a house where they could start a family.

Anna realized that Robert's attempts to influence her were simply his subconscious effort to prove that she could be a grown woman and mother, because the projection from her magnet was contradicting that. As soon as Anna decided to be an adult woman, Robert sensed this—and his need to change her vanished.

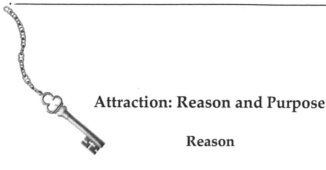

Attraction: Reason and Purpose

Reason

The force of your magnet attracts not only similar things, but also people who are looking for what you project outwardly. They are attracted to you because your projection promises certain experiences and feelings.

Your projection is made up of your feelings, which are the result of your experiences and your view of reality.

Purpose

◆ The purpose of mutual attraction is for people to "recognize" each other beyond the normal senses of perception, so that they can go on to experience certain situations together.
◆ For both people, the deeper purpose of every encounter is always to grow and learn more about themselves and others.

Putting the First Secret into Practice

◆ Think about some important events and people in your past. How did you grow through these life-changing encounters? Afterward, did you continue to attract similar things or was the pattern changed?

◆ Look at people in your circle of acquaintances who have become friends or partners. Let's assume it was not just because they enjoy each other's company, but because they wanted to experience something specific together. What experiences do they help each other have, and who plays which roles? Who is able to grow through which events, and who seems to be stuck right now?

◆ Observe the people who attract your attention for one reason or another. What are they trying to attract to their lives through their clothing, their behavior, or their status symbols? What do you think they are longing for when they do whatever it is that caught your eye?

How to Reset Your Magnet

◆ Once you understand and observe how events and people respond to one another, you will have a new view of reality. After experiencing the power of your magnet, you will want to start consciously changing it and putting it to good use. This knowledge will alter what you project and make you a much more active participant in shaping your own life.

◆ Imagine your "internal switch," and mentally flip it to your ideal projection as often as you want. Don't make any other changes—just watch and see what happens.

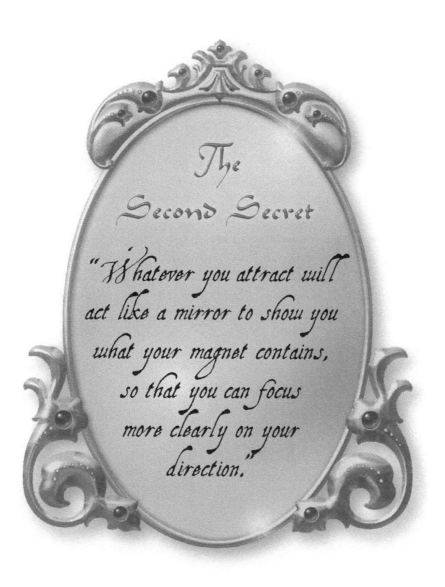

The
Second Secret

"Whatever you attract will
act like a mirror to show you
what your magnet contains,
so that you can focus
more clearly on your
direction."

The Mirror

The people and events that you have attracted into your life reflect the important parts of your magnet—they are like a mirror. This "mirror" principle doesn't mean that everyone you attract is just like you, rather it means that the people you attract reflect what is in your magnetic heart.

Individuals who hear about this concept sense that it could be true, but after a few attempts they stop trying to apply it because sometimes it seems to work and sometimes it doesn't. They fail to recognize the underlying principle, which is that the mirror doesn't just reflect who you are—it reveals much more! By observing events carefully, you can recognize exactly what your magnet is doing. As soon as you discover the reasons for these events behind circumstances, you can exert an influence on them.

Your magnetic heart works
in four different ways.
It can attract similar things, opposite things,
things you reject, and "miracles."

"You attract similar or equivalent things,
or you feel attracted by similar
or equivalent things."

When you draw a person into your life who shares many similarities with you, it feels good. You immediately understand why you found each other. Similarities feel familiar, and familiarity creates a sense of safety, security, and peace—feelings that most of us seek out.

"You're like me in many ways. I think that's wonderful." In those moments, you recognize yourself—you see a "kindred spirit." Because they are similar to you, you not only feel love for the other person but also love for yourself. You see and feel yourself in the other person. That's the first effect of the mirror.

Every time you find a similarity,
you recognize yourself.
And every time you decide to love
the other person for it,
you love yourself a little bit more.

*"You attract your opposite,
or you feel attracted by things that are your opposite."*

When the person you have attracted is very different from yourself, you might wonder why you ended up together. After all, he or she gives you less of that feeling of familiarity, understanding, and security than a person who has very similar qualities.

There are two reasons for this type of attraction. A very different person can either be a wonderful complement to your qualities or a constant provocation. Sometimes it's both, which creates a relationship that is either lively or unbearable, depending on the balance. In any case, when you are with this kind of person, you recognize what complements you, what you long for, and what you don't like. Once again, you gain more clarity about who you are.

When you notice a difference between you and another person, you sense where you yourself stand. Each time, you can decide how you want to grow— and this only adds to your strength.

24

"You attract exactly what you are trying to avoid."

When something—a type of person or a specific situation—constantly turns up in your life despite your best attempts to avoid it, it is simultaneously annoying *and* a perfect opportunity to find out which parts of your magnet are causing it. Undesirable repetitions are the clearest signposts. They show you where a pattern has become self-perpetuating and is now operating harmfully, rather like an undetected computer virus.

You strongly attract the things you have rejected because they awaken strong feelings and ideas in you—and these passionate parts of your magnet captivate other people.

To use another image: It is as though you were creating a film in your head. The film might be short and blurry at first, showing up as a few black-and-white images without sound. Gradually, the more experiences you have with that particular difficulty, the more extensive the script on "reject this issue" becomes. Your film grows longer and more detailed, color and sound get added. In time it can become a widescreen picture, and you might attract crowds of visitors who are looking for that exact movie because, on an emotional level, they want to experience the same story—with you in the starring role!

Three days before his fortieth birthday, Bill met Janet, a thirty-seven-year-old woman who lived close by. Bill had spent the previous year working intensively on his image of a soul mate, and Janet didn't seem to fit that picture. Many things about her were so different from the women he had dated in the past that he quickly ruled out the possibility of a romantic relationship. Freed from the pressure of becoming a couple, the two spent a great deal of time together and enjoyed discovering their differences.

One evening, Bill was lying in bed going over the past few days in his mind. Suddenly, in the middle of all the pleasant memories and feelings, the thought occurred to him: "What if she's the one after all?" If their time together felt this good, it might mean Janet was the woman he was looking for.

The next time they got together, Bill looked at Janet with fresh eyes; he started to think of her as a potential partner. In the process, he saw qualities that he had not noticed before. He also found himself admiring Janet's long black hair, her mysterious dark eyes, her slim graceful hands...and suddenly he was a goner. Bill began to feel clearly that Janet was the woman he had always dreamed about.

Janet didn't notice any of this at first, and as they became physically closer, Bill took it to mean that she shared his feelings. After a while, though, Janet turned the conversation to their relationship one evening and told Bill that she was very fond of him, but she couldn't imagine him as a romantic partner. He didn't want to believe it at first. The past few weeks had been wonderful for him. Bill started to look for reasons why it wasn't working out, and soon believed he had found one. He read in a book that a few combinations of astrological signs made a partnership extremely difficult—if not impossible. He researched various sources and kept finding confirmation on his theory: As a Pisces, Janet was the most unsuitable partner that he—a Libra—could possibly find.

From that point on, Bill saw Janet as a woman he had intense feelings of love and desire for but who could never be his life partner. Whenever he was with her, he saw what he could not possess and knew that he had laid the foundation for the worst possible lovesickness, but there was nothing he could do about it.

The relationship took its course over the year, with all of the usual highs and lows, until they finally separated for good. Bill swore that he would never experience so much drama again, and that he would never be attracted to another Pisces.

However, the next three women he felt attracted to were also Pisces! Bill learned about the secret of the heart magnet and realized he was attracting exactly what he was trying to avoid, but there was nothing he could do about it. In fact, his desire to avoid repeating this romantic drama had become so overpowering that on an online dating site he chose seven out of ten women who were Pisces based upon their pictures alone.

In another book, Bill read that love and acceptance were the quickest way to find healing. In his case, it was the only way he could see moving forward. He decided to stop fighting his intuition and his emotions, and to love himself for being interested in these women (despite their sign).

After another five months, he met Kate. They were almost magnetically attracted to each other, and Bill discovered that his intuition was still going strong: Kate was also a Pisces! By now he knew all of the qualities ascribed to this sign and he was pleased that he could recognize them one after the other in Kate. She was amazed by his understanding and tolerance—more than any other man had ever shown her. Now they live together.

Often, to break free from repetitive cycles, people are advised to focus intensively on what they want rather than on what they don't want. That's the fastest and easiest approach—when it works. When it isn't successful, which is true in most cases, it's because the rejection of the issue is still very much present. Even if you suppress it and cover it up with other desires, it remains stronger than the other forces in the magnet.

Every thought and feeling that you use to reject or judge another person or thing causes your magnet to attract it even more strongly.

At this point, you might be thinking that it's all well and good to know about this connection, but that it's impossible to suppress or control those internal processes in the long run—and you're absolutely right! Even if some people manage to do it, it's not a good idea to try to control your feelings and thoughts all the time—unless you're planning on being a Zen monk.

The Gentle Approach

There is an approach consisting of four simple steps that will help you fundamentally alter the "attracting what you reject" aspect of your magnet. The nice thing about this process, unlike many others, is you don't need to manage anything or change yourself at all. Nor do you need to "get things under control" or "organize your life"—you are a wonderful, magical person who is already in control. There are just a couple of ideas or images in your magnet that keep producing the same film....

This gentle technique will carefully help you shape a new projection for your magnet, with minimal effort on your part.

Step 1: Observe
Don't try to control anything, simply notice what is happening. You know how your thoughts, your feelings, and your magnet work together, and you may be aware of it as events transpire. Or you may not notice it much of the time—that's normal and completely fine.

Still, more and more frequently you will find that you "wake up" for a moment and become attuned to what's going on: "There's that thought again, and it's creating emotions to try and program my magnet." Or, "There's that situation or that type of person/behavior that my magnet always attracts. It's interesting how that works!"

The more clearly you see these effects, the less power a specific feeling of rejection will have. That's enough to start transforming your magnetic heart.

Step 2: Understand
The better you comprehend why things in your life happened in a particular way, the more you will feel okay about it. It might have been unpleasant, but that's a part of life. Are you completely sure, without a doubt, that events *needed* to be different? Everyone—including you—does whatever he or she needs to do because there is no other choice at that moment. If you could have done something differently, you would have. Understanding this will help you accept circumstances—and accepting them will help you to love. After a short while, you will notice which rejected thoughts continually resurface and create strong emotions. Even if the circumstances of your life have not changed, it is still helpful to observe which thoughts keep churning around in your head. These are completely irrelevant to your life. What's the point of an idea that is never followed by a discovery, an act, a movement, or a change? It's nothing more than ballast. If you happen to find one of these ruminations and observe it for a while, see whether you feel like getting rid of it. Remember: It will go away eventually, even if you don't do anything, because now

you understand how it works. Still, if you feel like you want to do something about it right away, try the following step.

Step 3: Accept

Accepting something internally is much easier than you might think. Acceptance is not the same as deciding that something is great, or even OK. It doesn't mean you have to love a circumstance or that you need to eliminate it, either. It just means seeing it for what it is and realizing that you're still a wonderful, lovable person—even with the issue.

If you can internally accept the reality
without fighting it, you will see the truth.
You won't avoid looking at it anymore.
And when you stop trying to avoid something,
your magnet will stop attracting it.

"I am just the way I am right now. Sad, happy, fearful, euphoric, shy, wounded, emotional, wistful...." That's the truth. Acceptance simply means seeing the truth in this moment—recognizing that everyone in the world has his or her own issues in life, and that it's absolutely fine because it's part of being human. It's normal. You may even find that these imperfections, both large and small, are what you appreciate about another person. And maybe, as you come to love them in another, you will find that you love the exact same things about yourself.

Step 4: Decide

These repetitive or negative thoughts won't just disappear now that you know about this power of acceptance. However, they will become less frequent and less powerful once you realize: "The more I keep thinking this, the more I seem to be magically attracting it. Is that what I want? No! What could I be thinking about instead? Ways to improve it, maybe?"

There might be a delay between your recognition and any external effects—meaning that despite your newfound clarity, you will still keep encountering the same undesired events or types of people for a while. In those moments, you are looking at your own past—but at least you will know why it is happening, which will make their attraction to your magnet weaker and weaker.

Clara and the Dinner

Clara is an employee at a technology company. After a series of "bad" romantic experiences, she no longer had the energy to start a new relationship. But one day, she got to know her co-worker Peter, and they planned a date to cook dinner at Clara's apartment. The evening started out well; the meal preparation was a success, and Clara felt good about it. She sent Peter into the dining room with two bowls of food while she tidied up in the kitchen. When she joined him a minute later, she was shocked—Peter had already started eating! That would have been unusual enough, since most men would surely wait for their hostess on a first date. But in Clara's case, there was another factor affecting her reaction: Her father had done the exact same thing to her mother all of his life. Clara had seen it as a child and had sensed her father's disrespect for his wife. For Clara, starting to eat before your partner had even come to the table was a terrible symbol of a loveless relationship.

She talked to Peter about it and learned that he had no problem with the situation because his parents had done the same thing. A lively debate ensued, and in the end Peter accused Clara of being immature.

The evening turned out to be much less romantic than planned. However, Clara still liked Peter, so they had two more dates. Each time, the discussion turned to their problems, and Clara didn't know how to respond. Finally, she had an idea that she shared with Peter. She imagined a space called the "problem-free zone," and they agreed to pretend that they were inside this area during their future dates. It worked! Whenever one of them wanted to talk about a problem, they considered whether they really wanted to disrupt the zone or contribute to a pleasant atmosphere instead. They still discussed their issues, but only outside the zone during nondate times. In the end, Clara and Peter didn't become a couple, but they did develop a strong friendship.

"You attract something inexplicable,
surprising, and new. You might call it a miracle."

Every time something miraculous happens, it shakes your belief in what you thought you knew about yourself and your life so far. You try to understand the miracle, but it's impossible to grasp. All you can do is accept it as a gift. At that instant, you might feel how much the universe loves you. Even if you can't comprehend it right away, there was still something in your magnet that attracted this blessing, or set it in motion.

Take a moment to think about one of those events in your life. Maybe you were trying hard to accomplish something. Maybe you were searching desperately for a partner, or you had been fighting for, or against, something for a long time. Perhaps you were trying hard to convince another person of something. Do you remember how it felt, and how tough and complicated everything seemed? The more you worked at it, the more difficult it felt. When you finally decided it was pointless to keep going, when you had already given up and were about to accept the idea that your life would go on even if you didn't get what you wanted—that's exactly when it happened. And it came about in a completely different way than you thought was possible.

At that point, you probably experienced an unusual internal state. You were probably happy and, in some sense, relieved. You had most likely let go of something—perhaps a person or an obsessive idea. You probably gave up trying to force the issue, not out of spite or anger, and not because you felt inadequate or victimized. To some extent, you simply handed it over to the universe because you realized there was nothing more you could do.

Do you love miracles? Put a feeling of surrender into your magnet and let go of your expectations. If you must expect something, simply expect a miracle.

If you can remember the feeling you had when you handed your issue over to the universe to be resolved, you will experience the exact same emotion that attracted the positive results.

This is described as "surrender." You did everything humanly possible, and then you let it go. You recognized your boundaries and perhaps sensed where a higher power took over—beyond your ability to influence it through your desires and actions alone.

According to many learned scholars from every culture and epoch, this line marks the entryway to the divine. It is your choice how you define it. What's important is that you recognize how it feels, because that will allow you to reset your magnet whenever you find yourself in a seemingly hopeless situation. Miracles happen when we let go. When we stop fighting for something that we thought we needed to achieve, something completely unexpected often happens. It appears as if by miracle, but it was attracted by your magnetic heart—just like everything else.

One of the best examples is the miracle of love. Love can only exist between two people when it is not forced. Control prevents love. If you truly let go, you will create the space for another person to love you, and for you to love your own life.

The Mirror: Reason and Purpose

Reason

- The people around you, and their actions, are not coincidental. On some level, you either sought them out, they sought you out, or a little bit of both.
- The people and situations in your life reflect underlying causal factors within your heart magnet. You can purposely work to strengthen those elements that cause positive events, and to eliminate those with negative results.

Purpose

- The purpose of the events and people you attract is to discover who you are and where you stand right now, and to decide the direction you want your life to take next.
- The mirror reflects what your magnet has attracted in the past so that you can utilize the knowledge to consciously make new decisions.

Putting the Second Secret into Practice

- Look at the people who play a role in your life. Why did you attract them? In which ways do they strengthen, complement, or repel you?
- Observe the qualities you find among your friends and acquaintances. In what ways do they agree with you about things that are

important to you? How are they judgmental? Where are their views fixed? Who has characteristics that are fundamentally different from yours, and in what areas? The elements that create strong emotions within you indicate what you do and don't want. They give you clarity about yourself.

◆ Pay attention when someone gets upset about something. Often they are angry about their own mirror, which is reflecting the contents of their own magnet. Many times, people criticize the same qualities in others that they have and have not yet personally resolved.

◆ Look at people who are successful. How do they deal with their mirrors? How do they handle positive and negative events and encounters? Very often, these individuals are able to extract valuable lessons from every experience, and as a result, they can effortlessly correct the course of their lives and actions when needed.

How to Reset Your Magnet

Your magnet's effect will start to shift positively as soon as you use the mirror to discover why you attracted specific events, people, and behaviors in the past. Once you have identified the "issue," cause, and connections, you have already taken the first step toward change, because you have resolved an important part of the old attraction to the issue in question.

The Third Secret

"From the chaos of countless possibilities, your clarity draws out the exact people and events that best complement your life."

Clarity

The reality that surrounds you is filled with infinitely more possibilities than you can imagine, or even perceive. In short, *everything* exists—every kind of person and every kind of behavior. If you wanted to record and understand all of it, there wouldn't be any time left to live your actual life.

When you walk through a big shopping mall, it never occurs to you to look at every single item, let alone try to understand the function and structure of all the merchandise on display. Even when you are wandering around aimlessly, you predominantly notice the things that have something to do with you and your life.

Luckily, your job is not to understand everything. Your purpose is to sort through the endless possibilities and pick out the ones that resonate with your life plan. To that end, it's a good idea to have some sort of image in your mind of how you would like your world to look and feel. You might call this your "life idea."

Who are you? Where do you want to go? What do you desire most? What do you absolutely want to experience? What kind of people do you want to spend time with? What is the meaning of life for you—both at this moment and fundamentally?

These are not easy questions; even if you find the answers, they will always change over time. Fortunately, the point is not to find absolute or final answers but to develop a feel for the direction you want to go. This sense of the flow of your own life creates a clear, powerfully attractive magnet.

The Power of Longing

Let's assume that you live what many people would consider a "normal" life. You eat, drink, sleep, go to work, meet people, have a hobby, and sometimes take a vacation. It can be a truly wonderful life if you love it just the way it is. Such a life can be paradise—as long as you don't feel like something is missing.

But if you do feel something is missing—what exactly is that "something"? Most likely, it is an unfulfilled longing.

Longing is one of the strongest forces in your magnet. This energy can bring you all of the things you desire—or it can prevent you from getting them.

The force of your longing is a double-edged sword. Your aching desire can lead you forward in life—to create something—or it can nearly destroy you if it goes unfulfilled. It is the same force, but what it does is up to you.

You don't necessarily need to reach a specific goal to satisfy your longing. Above all, your longing shows you what kinds of emotions you want to experience.

Many people feel a sense of longing when they see sailboats on the ocean. They fantasize about adventure and far-off lands. Mostly, they dream about freedom. Some people decide to fulfill this desire. They work hard for many years to save the money they need to achieve this sense of freedom. During this time, they create even more limitations for themselves, and they postpone their happiness for the future.

As soon as you recognize that every longing is a desire to experience a certain feeling, you can decide whether you need to reach a specific external goal or if there is an alternative way to generate those same feelings in your life.

There's a simple way to use the power of an intense longing: Give it a channel through which it can flow and achieve something. For the sake of the forces of attraction in your magnet, it's important not to keep your longings locked away. What would you project if you were constantly painfully aware that something was missing? Dissatisfaction. If you want to attract satisfied people into your life, it's not beneficial to project this negative emotion.

*The best thing you can do for yourself
is to be clear about your life idea and
to feel like you are on the path
to your perfect future.*

What kinds of people are you most likely to attract if you don't have much clarity about your life idea?

- People who don't have a clear life idea of their own! This can be positive because your shared life can represent your purpose and fulfillment. On the other hand, it can also quickly become boring, unfulfilling, and tense. That's because you are not growing, balancing, or complementing each other.
- People who think it's great that you don't have a life idea, because then they can easily manipulate you to fit into their own plan. Does that sound familiar? How long can you stand to be a part of someone else's life idea and not your own?
- No one at all, because you've already experienced the first and second scenarios and you won't let it happen again. Additionally, the type of person you're looking for—someone with clear ideas— will not be attracted to you because he or she is looking for a partner who has clarity like they do in order to fulfill his or her longings.

"Your happiness in life depends upon the quality of your thoughts."

Marcus Aurelius
Roman emperor
121–180 AD

The Power of Your Thoughts

When it comes to shaping your future, people often say that the power of your thoughts, hopes, and ideas acts like a magnet to attract people and events into your life. However, your thoughts are not the only elements at work here—the feelings associated with certain ideas also play a significant role. Your thoughts are like an ignition key, while your feelings are the actual engine.

You may have already read or heard about the power of wishing. You maybe even tried it but gave up after your initial excitement and a few small successes because it wasn't meeting your expectations.

If the wishing hasn't worked for you in the past, there are three probable reasons:

Roadblock #1: You Want to Have Something

Why? Often because you feel like something is missing. You sense a lack. At first, you have an enormously positive feeling because you're excited that your desires might be fulfilled. Your inner child has discovered a new game. It's exactly the right starting point for your magnetic heart. But if your wishes don't come true when and how you want them, your inner child loses its enthusiasm. You might become listless, disappointed, and angry with the people who suggested this pointless activity. You might decide that the entire process is completely absurd.

A beautiful thought without feelings is like a flower without water—it quickly loses its power and beauty. And when it is no longer beautiful, you no longer notice it.

Roadblock #2: You Can See the Goal but It's Far Away

Yes, it's good to imagine your goal as vividly as possible. However, there is often a feeling of distance between you and the final destination. You realize that you haven't achieved it yet. You feel separate from your goal, and that negatively affects your heart magnet.

Let's imagine you were advised to look at expensive houses, even though you don't have the money to buy one. Or to test drive your dream car even though you haven't the faintest idea how you would finance it.

These activities will create a strong attraction in your magnetic heart, as long as you also have the feeling that you're "on your way." You don't need to know the entire path in detail. In fact, you don't even need to know how the results will come to you, as long as you truly feel you are on the right track.

If you don't feel like you are on the path to attaining your goals, that's probably the reason for the roadblock. Most people don't enjoy having rewards dangled in front of them if there's little to no chance of actually receiving them.

Roadblock #3: It's Important to You
This may sound familiar: Often, when something isn't important, you accomplish it very easily. But as soon as you become invested in the outcome of a situation, everything goes wrong, or at least you experience some unpleasant feelings and a great deal of anxiety. Assigning too much value to a situation is a roadblock that prevents you from being playful. If you tell yourself to build a sand castle—but then add that it needs to look a certain way and be done immediately—the creative process loses its fun factor.

"The path is the goal."

Confucius
Founder of Confucianism
551–479 BC

Power Without Effort: Intention, Path, and Joy

 The First Decisive Power:
Having an Intent Rather Than a Wish

Instead of simply wishing to have a partner in your life, decide to have one! Don't talk to others about your desires. If you share at all, tell them what you have *decided* to have. Isn't it a freeing thought? Can you feel the difference? It's as if a burden has been lifted from your shoulders. That's the feeling of intention we're looking for here. When you wish for something, it often comes with the feeling that you need to "do" something—that you need to wish "correctly," "make things right," or simply wait. The process of wishing often involves the unconscious idea that someone or something has to come along to fulfill it. As a result, you're dependent on that event.

By contrast, if you "decide to have it," you have already set the wheels in motion. You don't need to worry about it or fix it, nor do you need to wait. It has been set in motion because you made the decision. Where there was previously a lack of something, or a void, there is now a path.

 The Second Decisive Power:
Paying Attention to the Path, Not Just the Goal
Imagine you're going to meet a friend to go to the movies or your favorite restaurant tomorrow night. Doesn't it feel like you're already on your way there? Like it's coming toward you? There's no doubt that you're going to do it. Even if something unexpected came up, you would simply adjust your schedule a little.

That's the feeling of being "on the path." You sense that three things have come together as one: you in the present moment, your goal, and the path to your goal. Once you feel this oneness, you don't need to worry about how you're going to reach your destination.

You can become one with...

◈ the feeling of having your future partner by your side. With the feeling that your two life paths are inevitably moving toward one another, and with the sense of being present together in the here and now, at this point on your life's journey.
◈ your future job, where you will feel as comfortable as if you were at a friend's house. Comfortable with the feeling of moving toward it, and comfortable with yourself, here and now.

◆ your perfect vacation. All of the actions you will bring to this exact spot. And with the present you.

◆ the feeling of how you've always wanted to live. Your life at this moment (not as a permanent state, but as an intermediate stop). And with yourself, here and now.

Doesn't it feel like everything is right, because you're always on your way toward your goals?

 The Third Decisive Power:
Feeling the Joy Instead of the Weight of Important
Things

When you decide to go to the movies to see a wonderful film, or when you find a great restaurant to enjoy your favorite dish...is that "important"? Is it "significant" to your life? Or are you doing it because it's fun?

Of course there are situations that are very stressful, and nothing is more natural than the desire to change them. But the more importance we give to these circumstances, the more we suffer. Dealing with this suffering saps all the strength we could be using to create a fulfilling future.

There are ways to lessen the weight of important events and situations, so that you can be free to feel a sense of joy about creating something new:

◆ Imagine yourself, looking back at your current problem ten or twenty years from now: Is this moment or this goal really so important in the context of your entire life?

◆ Is it really true that you will be happy if you reach this one particular goal? Not just somewhat happy or possibly happy, but truly happy? Can you say this with absolute certainty? What you are longing or striving for right now—if you are fully honest with yourself—is actually just an attempt to see if something will work. Trying something out is fun; "needing" it is not.

◆ Do you have a backup plan? It's reassuring to have an idea of what you would do with your life if you were unable to reach your goal. Maybe your plan is not going to fail, because you can feel that you are already on the right path, but even if it did, it wouldn't be a disaster. You're always free to explore new options in the universe. That's part of the adventure, and the reason that you're here. Finding alternatives in the game of life—that's the power of backup plans.

Look Out—It's a Trap!

How Your Wishes Affect Other People

The wonderful tool of "wishing" can mean that a potential partner is drawn to you as if by magic. As soon as such a person comes into your life, you need to change your wish fulfillment approach right away, or you might not get your desired results! Don't make the individual the star of your "internal film" while you're still in the early phase of getting to know each other. Of course it's very tempting to do so, but let's take a look at what might happen if you do:

In the First Step...

...of attracting a suitable partner, devote as much time as possible to your fantasy of how you want to feel when you're with the right person. Don't worry about external characteristics—just focus on feeling, as if the person were already with you. At the same time, feel like you're already on your way to finding this partner. That will create a strong magnetic field within your heart that will attract people with similar desires.

In the Second Step...

...a person with the same feelings as yours comes into your life. At first, you will be excited about the similarities and shared ideals that created the attraction. A wonderful period of mutual discovery begins. Up until now, everything has been picture perfect.

In the Third Step...

...you often find yourself thinking about a future with this person. You have already found many ideal qualities in her or him, so it makes sense to believe the rest of the person will suit you perfectly as well. Simultaneously, part of you starts to suspect that not everything is perfect. Because this suspicion threatens your dream and creates an unpleasant feeling, you suppress it.

In the Fourth Step...

...you create an idealized image of the other person, known as a *projection*. You project your own love story onto the other person as if onto a movie screen. You no longer see your romantic interest as he or she really is. Naturally you're only projecting good thoughts and feelings, but this can be problematic. The other person will intuitively sense this unsolicited projection on your part and will find it uncomfortable.

Imagine if you meet a potential partner but you need some time to understand your own emotions. How would you feel if you knew that the other person had already mentally made you a permanent part of his or her future?

Your reaction might even feel physical—often described as restrictive, suffocating, or even threatening. People feel pressure in their chests, a tightness in their throats, and the inexplicable desire to flee.

You can now see how a well-meaning thought that originates from your sense of being in love can actually cause the opposite of what you desire.

*Wish for as much as you can
and expect the best.
And stop as soon as
a specific person is involved!*

What's Better?

Especially when you're in love, it seems like a superhuman task to avoid thinking about your shared future. You've spent much too long wishing this person into your life to waste time on doubts and questions now. If the attraction is developing more or less equally on both sides, it's much less of a problem than in a situation where one person is still hesitant. If you were still unsure, how would you want the other person to act?

It would probably be nice if the other person kept to him- or herself for a bit and gave your relationship time and space to grow. Love cannot be rushed—it must unfold naturally. If you try to force the bud of a flower to open before it is ready, it will not blossom. As soon as you start putting pressure on love to grow, you destroy it. You've waited so long already...are a couple more weeks really going to matter?

The best thing you can do to let
mutual feelings bloom is to not do
anything in particular.
Feelings need space and time.

In practice, everyone knows that things aren't always so easy, especially when your own feelings are developing quickly. Sometimes it helps to imagine that you're conducting an experiment: "What will the universe do if I don't try to convince the other person that I'm the right one?" It means fundamentally trusting in your own life, having faith that everything happens for the best in the end. You might think about your last long relationship. How did you first get together? Didn't it seem to happen organically, somehow? You can be sure of one thing: If you and the new person in your life are meant to be together, it will happen on its own again. And if not, you can rest assured that your attempts to force the relationship wouldn't have made it any better.

"Life is not a problem to be solved, but a reality to be experienced."

Siddhartha Gautama, Buddha
Enlightened teacher and founder of Buddhism
563–483 BC

Lovesickness: A Few Remedies

Don't try *not* to love. It's impossible, and it only causes pain. It is okay to love, even when it's not reciprocated. Love fully, with every fiber of your being, even if your love might never be returned. Then, at least the suppressed feeling can't hurt you, only the destruction of the illusion of having a relationship with the object of your affection.

Don't try to "let go" of someone, as it is not something you can simply resolve to do. It happens on its own—or it doesn't. Instead, try to recall your earlier ideal life path prior to your relationship with this individual. Remember how you really want to feel.

Find out exactly which part of your heart magnet attracted the other person. Once you understand the secret of your magnetic heart, you will be able to redirect its destructive power in order to find love.

Anger mainly comes about because you feel helpless and subject to another person's actions. It can be beneficial to look at the points where your two life paths don't match up, and start creating a new, even clearer course for yourself.

Patrick's Pilgrimage

The story of Patrick, a fifty-six-year-old insurance agent, shows how reliably the secret of the magnetic heart works. He and his wife separated when he was fifty, after more than twenty-five years of marriage and two children. The reason behind the split was Patrick's longing for a kind of life that he felt he had been suppressing in order to be a good father and husband.

Patrick wanted the freedom to travel and to experience affairs with different women. So he bought himself a one-way ticket to South America.

On the surface, it seemed like Patrick was living exactly the way he had always imagined: He indulged in adventures in foreign countries, along with the occasional romantic liaison. The image he had desired during his unfulfilled years of marriage had been very clear, and that's exactly what he got.

He should have been a happy man, but Patrick had an unresolved internal conflict: He suffered from feelings of loneliness. Often, his longing for company was so overwhelming that he had to go out in the middle of the night to be around other people. This traveler was constantly searching for companions who could give him physical intimacy—at the very least. Again and again Patrick encountered women who also suffered from loneliness or a fear of commitment. They reflected his own inner turmoil, so even when he was lying next to someone, he felt the same loneliness.

Finally, the spiral of loneliness and seeking out women became so intense and painful that Patrick nearly committed suicide. Deeply affected by his loss of control, he decided to pull the emergency brake on his destructive behavior. This troubled man took a vow to avoid intimate contact for one entire year. Simultaneously, he began a new pilgrimage that he had mapped out for himself. He visited monasteries and spiritual teachers from various cultures, tried out different paths and faiths, and finally discovered Sufism—a teaching of Islam.

Here his vow and his suffering found a home, because one of the rules he was given was abstinence. After a few months, Patrick returned home and went back to his old job. Because Sufism only permits intimate contact within marriage, Patrick decided he wanted to find a new wife.

He placed a personal ad in the local paper, consisting of just two lines: "Male, 56, following the Sufi path, wishes to marry. If this speaks to you, please contact me."

Patrick's friends made bets that no one would respond, but a week later he received a message from a woman who wanted to meet him. When they met in a café, they were both equally smitten. They talked for hours about anything and everything. Not once did the conversation turn to Patrick's faith, which—as he learned later—the woman had never heard of before.

When Patrick asked the woman about her interests and life path, he learned that she was about to be certified as a Tantric yoga instructor. With incredible precision, Patrick's magnetic heart had attracted exactly the kind of person his logical mind never would have chosen—but she was the type of person he had always emotionally longed for. Their mutual attraction was so strong that they went back to Patrick's *house after the date and experienced one of the most magical nights of love he had ever known.*

Patrick solved the problem of abstinence, which his new faith required, in a very down-to-earth way. He married his beloved inwardly and quietly, within his own heart.

Definitively rejecting something in yourself—and in your own life—creates one of the strongest magnetic forces possible. Your mind is constantly working to create an image that produces intense feelings to attract others. In Patrick's case, once he stopped rejecting his previous notions about freedom, and he found a new, clear intention, the tiny ad was enough to attract the right feelings and the right person.

Rejecting negative behaviors and thoughts from your life creates one of the strongest forces in your magnetic heart. Your mind and heart are constantly working to project an image about who you are in order to attract the people around you. In Patrick's case, once he made the commitment to Sufism and changed his lifestyle, he was able to attract the perfect person.

Clarity and Longing: Reason and Purpose

Reason

- If you know what feelings you want to experience, you will send out clear signals, and people will respond to them.
- Your clarity about who you are and what you want will help you sort through a large number of possible feelings to find exactly the ones that suit you, thus programming your heart magnet.
- If, despite your sense of clarity, you don't attract what you want, it is because the pull of an opposing emotion is stronger—either a fear of, or a simultaneous desire for, a contrasting feeling.

Purpose

- The purpose of a longing is to show you the path to the feelings that you want to experience. The specific event that causes you to experience these is not important.
- People who have similar longings attract one another. Sometimes they want to experience the same feeling together, but ultimately, they just want to find each other.

Putting the Third Secret into Practice

◆ Where do you feel unfulfilled longings in yourself? Write them down! Which desires will truly give you strength to create something new? Which ones are negatively affecting your happiness? What feelings do you want to experience? What are some other ways to achieve them? Ask yourself these questions and see how your attitude toward life changes.

◆ Look at people whose lives seem to be easy and who create a positive atmosphere when you get together with them. They all have something in common: They feel good about their lives. They know what they want. They don't put a lot of energy into rejection—they simply let troubling issues go. These individuals don't get attached to—or obsess about—specific problems. Instead, they focus on what interests them. This clarity is the key to their success.

◆ Look at people who strongly reject something or who have a narrow worldview. Observe the conditions of their personal lives and what kinds of careers they pursue. You will notice that their environment has responded in a predictable way.

How to Reset Your Magnet

Clarity comes from knowing yourself and recognizing the power and effects of your decisions.

◆ You will find increasing clarity the more you know about what sort of lifestyle makes you happy. Create a vision of how you want to feel, independent of other people and how they act.

◆ Realize that everything you do is preceded by a decision.

◆ Recognize that even when you're not doing anything, you're making a decision: the decision not to do anything. Even if you believe you're powerless—a victim of circumstances or obligation—you are making the choice to believe that.

◆ Decisions can only affect your magnet if your heart shares in the decision. In case of doubt, wait until both your heart and mind say yes. Don't make decisions that contradict how you feel.

61

The Fourth Secret

"The source of everything
you seek lies
within your heart magnet.
The source is
what you feel."

Your Own Source

No one acts solely on the basis of reason. On a deeper level, the goal is always to experience a certain feeling. Even when people claim to be making decisions based upon rationale and logic, they are often doing so because it gives them a feeling of emotional security, for instance. It allows them to understand their actions, explain them, look at the results, and justify them. It reduces the risk of being punished for a possible mistake, which would feel unpleasant.

The Goal Is Always to Experience Feelings
Logically speaking, it doesn't make any sense for a mountain climber to climb a peak or for an explorer to cross the desert. Similarly, it's completely irrelevant how quickly a racecar driver can go or how creative an artist is. But these drives or desires are understandable when you know about the power of emotions. Even in professions where you wouldn't expect it, the deeper reason for every action is the longing to experience a feeling.

◆ A politician doesn't campaign for an issue because of the issue itself, but because he or she wants to experience certain feelings in relation to the issue: the feeling of "doing the right thing," for example; the feeling of having a purpose in life; the emotional security of forming an opinion; the feeling of belonging to a community (the political party); asserting him- or herself in order to feel empowered....

◆ A computer programmer doesn't write programs as a "technical" exercise but because he or she is looking for specific emotional experiences: Being conscious of his or her own intelligence; the pleasure that comes from solving a problem; the feeling of being useful to others; the feeling of achieving something and having situations under control (in other words, not being a victim)....

◆ A high-level manager wants to feel the joy of winning, asserting him- or herself, creating material security, and exercising power. Without the feelings promised by such a position, the work wouldn't offer much motivation.

"Reason shapes the man, but emotion guides him."

Jean-Jacques Rousseau
French–Swiss writer, teacher, composer,
and social and political theorist
1712–1778 AD

As mentioned previously, the driving force behind everything we do is the desire to attain certain feelings or emotions. Our rational mind is only an instrument that helps us accomplish this, though it sometimes tricks us into thinking that it is the reason we do what we do.

On a day-to-day basis, many people live without experiencing the feelings that they long for—particularly in their professional lives. An entire life lived like this would have no meaning. The more someone ignores the feelings that they truly want to experience, the more meaningless their life becomes, and the more they attempt to fill this void by seeking such feelings from—and through—others. Projecting such neediness from your magnet is a less-than-ideal way to attract fulfilling partnerships and friendships.

The Power of Your Own Source

Whatever it is that you seek from another person, know that you already carry it within yourself. After all, what is it that you're really looking for—feelings! Feelings of security, of being loved, abundance, freedom, being part of a family, success....

No one can *give* you a feeling. They can only awaken one already within you. Feelings belong to you, and only you can produce them.

66

The people surrounding you are a gift meant to help you achieve this. This knowledge is of key importance. If you recognize that your emotions are yours alone, and that not a single one can be given or taken by another person, then you will be set free. You will grant others less power over you and, in the process, assume responsibility for your own well-being. This leaves less room for blaming others—a practice that only makes difficult situations worse.

No one can give you love, because the love resides within you. Observe an animal or plant or something else in nature that touches you. Can you feel the love within yourself? Look at a picture of a happy child. Can you feel the happiness? You haven't been "given" anything from outside your being, yet you can still feel it. It's the same love that you feel when someone who you adore is near you.

If you have a problem with someone,
you cannot control their contribution
to the issue. You can only change your part—
and maybe then, theirs will also disappear.

The Difficult Path of Those Who Seek Love

When people are looking for certain feelings but cannot find anything to fulfill them—or when they have lived without love for a long time—they sometimes start to develop behaviors that others find strange or confusing. Ultimately, it is always a cry for love.

"I'm successful, I'm hard-working, I'm beautiful, I'm intelligent, I have a job, I have a house, I have this and that...."

The harder someone tries to demonstrate all of this, the louder he or she is really shouting, "Please like me. Please love me!"

Others portray the victim: "I'm lonely, I'm sick, I'm poor, I'm weak, I'm not doing well. Please notice me. Please love me!"

The attempt to obtain positive feelings and confirmation from others is strenuous for everyone involved. Those seeking love in such a way are often only briefly valued for what they do or have—instead of who they really are.

"Don't forget that the best relationship is one where your love for each other is greater than your need for each other."

Tenzin Gyatso
The 14th Dalai Lama
Buddhist monk, Tibetan leader
1935–

The Simple Path of Love's Light
Don't go looking for light outside yourself; fill yourself with light, and others will take notice. If you know about the secret of your magnetic heart, it will be much easier to find what you're seeking. In doing so, you will be programming your magnet with the feelings that you want to attract to your life.

◆ If you want someone to open his or her heart to you...open your own first. They are your mirror—they can't do something that you're not able to do yourself. Even if they do open themselves first, you won't be able to feel it unless your heart is already open.

◆ If you want to improve your relationship with another person, improve your relationship with yourself.

◆ If you want to feel more trust, put more trust in yourself.

◆ If you want to feel more love, love yourself more.

◆ If you're looking for security, give yourself security.

◆ If you want to be better treated better, treat yourself better.

◆ If you want to experience wealth, give yourself a sense of self-fulfillment first. This doesn't take any money, just an adjustment in your attitude.

◆ If you're longing for new experiences, seek them out. Start with something small, and the bigger things will follow on their own.

◆ If you don't want others to judge you, first make sure that you're not judging yourself.

◆ If you want to be respected, respect yourself.

◆ If you want more freedom to make decisions and aren't given it, then simply make decisions for yourself.

The Perfect Compass: "How Do I Want to Feel?"
When you feel like a relationship is in a rut—regardless of which stage it is in—trying to "fix" the other person often makes it worse.

If you want to use the power of your magnetic heart, try this: Base your behavior upon the feeling that you want to experience. When you see a conflict arising, remember your goal and ask yourself, "Do I want to experience the feeling of what's about to transpire?" If you make your decision ahead of time, your answer will be clear.

Decide on a specific feeling
you want from life,
not a specific behavior.

One benefit of this strategy is that you can temporarily interrupt an escalating argument by realizing that the two of you are becoming more and more blinded by unwanted feelings. It doesn't mean that you are ignoring the problem. It just means that you aren't letting the issue take on a life of its own, or letting the negative feelings shape the situation. By deciding how you want to feel, you can regain control and successfully avert a downward spiral.

Another benefit of choosing a feeling is that arguments cannot affect it. Everyone has the right to feel good, and there are very few persuasive arguments against that.

 *Christina's Direction*

Christina, who works in marketing, spent many years looking for something that she called her "direction." After countless difficult attempts at romantic relationships—many of them with dramatic endings—she felt tired, resigned, and confused. She had never figured out why her relationships kept ending with a spontaneous loss of interest or rejection by the other person. Only after her intense experience with Henry did she finally realize that she hadn't been paying attention to the signals she had been receiving and projecting her entire life.

She met Henry, a Canadian manager, at an international conference. In addition to being physically attracted to him, she found his competent, self-assured attitude during his presentation particularly alluring. Christina had always been attracted to successful men, and Henry embodied her ideal more than any other.

They soon grew close, and after the conference they spent a weekend together at a resort. Christina earned a good living, but Henry still insisted on catering to her every desire at his own expense. She saw this as a sign of his affection and respect, and really enjoyed their time together.

When they met again two weeks later at another business event, they spent another intense weekend together. A part of Christina felt like she was in heaven—this man seemed to embody her ideal man—and yet there was something that troubled her. Henry told her that, despite how he felt about her, his career was the most important thing in his life. Christina was used to hearing this from successful men, and in some sense, that was exactly what she liked about Henry.

What was completely unfamiliar to her were the feelings that overwhelmed her one night as she lay next to her sleeping lover—anxiety so intense that it made her tremble, insomnia, and deep feelings of abandonment and loneliness. Christina's desire to flee from the situation was so intense that she got out of bed and spent several hours on the couch in the living room. Since Henry hadn't said or done anything to cause these emotions, Christina didn't mention them to him. How would she have explained it?

About two weeks after that troubling night, Henry cut off contact without any explanation. The relationship was over. Christina blamed herself and spent several days and nights searching for reasons why it had happened.

She confided in a close friend who had experienced something similar and who had found a solution for himself. He suggested that Christina take a short mental journey into the past. Christina once again pictured the situation in which she was lying next to Henry, wishing she could escape. This time, in her mind, she didn't suppress the urge but instead imagined packing her bags and driving home. Again and again she imagined doing this, and analyzed how it felt. She discovered that it would have been the right thing to do. This discovery, combined with the feelings she experienced during her imaginary journey, significantly eased her pain. She was able to think clearly again, which allowed her to look more closely for why her magnet had once again attracted a relationship with an abrupt ending.

Christina realized that she considered her own professional life so important that her magnet couldn't help but attract men who did the *same. She gave it so much importance that she wouldn't have been able to describe the purpose of her life without her career. The men she attracted were on the exact same life path.*

Christina was even more surprised when she realized that particularly intense, negative feelings toward another person are also a form of "direction." Such feelings don't mean that the other person is bad. The emotions simply point out that the two people's magnetic hearts differ in significant ways, causing a feeling of unease. The "direction" Christina had been seeking for so long was sending her a very clear message that night.

Many people experience situations like Christina's time and again, so it makes sense to look at what's really happening: You grow closer to a potential partner. Everything feels incredibly exciting and you become intimate quickly. It is very passionate and intense—it's a wonderful experience. Problems only arise if you suppress other feelings as they start to make themselves known. There's a reason they start to bubble up. The reason could be inside you—for instance, because the new relationship activates one of your unresolved issues and brings it to the surface. Or it could be that you are fundamentally mismatched, as in Christina's case.

Pay attention to whether any "drama" is building. If something doesn't feel quite right or maybe even feels bad, listen to it! Your feelings are your direction!
They know better than your mind.

The reason you experience emotions like Christina's when you are intimate with, or even just physically close to another person, is probably because your two magnetic hearts (energy fields) don't fit together. In a manner of speaking, they are causing a constant state of disruption, and you sense it in your body as well. Your feelings lead to unpleasant thoughts and intense questioning over the reasons why, which of course cannot be explained through conventional means. Since you can't find a solution, these thoughts create more and more negative feelings.

The more clearly you understand what feelings you want to experience in your life, the more clearly and certainly you will recognize what suits you and what doesn't.

"One drop of love is more than an ocean of reason."

Blaise Pascal
French mathematician, physicist, author, philosopher
1623–1662

Emotion and Reason

After a series of meaningless and fruitless arguments, a woman tells her partner, "You know, I chose you because you made me feel good. And now you're making me feel bad. I don't know why that is, what changed, or how we can solve it.

All I know is that I want to feel good, and you can't make it happen. And that makes me very sad."

As soon as she says that, the atmosphere instantly changes. Her partner realizes that his desire to win every debate will soon make him a loser, because he is about to irreparably damage—instead of heal—something that he values greatly.

When logical reason and illogical emotion are at war, reason usually wins. And reason is usually happy about it, not realizing that every victory is a step toward a greater loss, because at some point, emotion that is never allowed to be felt or heard will leave. And then it will feel like something has been lost forever.

Uncoupling: A Simple Emotional Exercise for Greater Freedom

Are you in a situation where you are bound up in another person's emotional world without wanting to be? Or is there someone you'd like to meet without any kind of emotional pressure, just to see what develops once the drama is taken out of the picture? If you like experiments, you might enjoy the following mirror-neuron game, which can immediately change the effects of your magnet and your relationship with another person. Take a few minutes for yourself, without disruptions, and try this:

1   Close your eyes. Feel yourself simply sitting there and breathing. Imagine the other person. Try to visualize a tube of light linking the two of you. That's the channel. Can you see it? Now imagine you have a giant, invisible pair of scissors, and mentally cut through the tube. You might need to make a few snips. Now observe whether you feel any difference. If not, that's okay—continue to the next step.

2   You might notice that half of the severed tube of light is still connected to you. There might also be a kind of cloud or patch of light hanging around the connection point (maybe your heart or your belly). Get rid of these remnants by saying out loud, "My goal is to send everything I'm observing right now back to X (the other person's first name)." Say it just like that, without any modifications. Then don't do anything—just wait. Finally, observe once again what is happening and how you feel.

You can do this exercise with anyone—with your partner, or even with relatives, if you want to improve your relationship. You aren't abandoning the person, and you're not cutting off your love. You're just getting rid of old history and useless negative emotions to create room for true love and baggage-free encounters in the here and now.

Your Own Source: Reason and Purpose

Reason

- Every feeling that you have radiates outwardly and attracts people who match that feeling.
- Feelings are often uncontrollable, but they are never accidental. The catalyst is sometimes external, but the source is always within you. Once you have found the catalyst, you can reset your magnet.

Purpose

- The purpose of knowing and using your own source is to learn more about yourself and to become more aware of your own strength.
- When you recognize your own source, you will be less bound to other people's feelings. This will allow you to love them even more—regardless of who they are and their actions.

Putting the Fourth Secret into Practice

❖ Observe your feelings when other people don't act the way you would like them to. How does it feel to be emotionally bound to another person?

❖ Observe how your relationships change after you practice the uncoupling exercise. You don't need to change your behavior—just observe.

❖ Notice what happens when you imagine giving yourself what you used to expect from others. Do you feel better or worse?

❖ Remember and observe other people's reactions when you feel good and when you feel bad.

How to Reset Your Magnet

◆ Explore your deep longings. If you have a recurring desire— maybe in the form of a dream—then try to discover what feelings it would help you experience. What does your dream stand for? What's behind it? As long as you aren't experiencing these feelings, their absence will negatively shape your magnet.

◆ Find out how else you might be able to experience these feelings, and practice this as much as possible.

◆ If you expect certain feelings from others, give those feelings to yourself.

This will help you switch your magnet from "unavailable" to "available," so that it finally attracts what you are seeking.

The Fifth Secret

"*Every time you find a symbol in your magnet, you hold a magical key for change in your hand.*"

The Power of Symbols

Faith in a specific symbol or behavioral ritual can provide a powerful kind of independent "programming" within your magnet. This kind of faith can support what you want to achieve, but it can also completely block it.

As long as you believe in a symbol, it will keep turning up in your life—or in your relationships—because it will attract people who sense it in your magnet and are unconsciously drawn to it. In cases where the symbol stands for an unpleasant memory, it will constantly bring you similar experiences.

Our mind is always searching for certainty and security. Because it likes to make things easy for itself, it uses objects and actions that it has already identified as symbolizing something as placeholders. At some point, it can no longer tell that they are just individual objects and actions that don't necessarily correspond to your present reality. As long as your magnet holds on to strong symbols that "unintentionally" spark feelings tied to past experiences, you will continue to reproduce an automatic response to the symbol itself, rather than reacting to the actual situation at hand.

Symbols as Language

Because symbols and rituals are a kind of language, good interpersonal relations require the speakers to have the same understanding of each "word." If you associate a feeling with an object or action, and then meet someone who doesn't know anything about these associations, you are laying the groundwork for problems.

◆ Symbols that have positive associations for you allow people to produce pleasant feelings in you if they use your symbol appropriately. This is great if the other person is doing this to express his or her true feelings. However, if he or she is manipulating the symbol to achieve a goal and is not genuine, this can be the basis for complications, misunderstandings, and drama.

◆ Symbols that have negative associations for you can recreate unpleasant memories and emotions. Even if the other person doesn't know anything about the symbol and considers it to be neutral, or is trying to use it to express loving feelings, it can spark a negative response within you. In this case, your symbol is causing a new, potentially positive encounter to wither before it can bloom.

An object or an action stands for something.
You've experienced it yourself,
and anyone can see it.
But is it absolutely true? Always?

Common Symbols and Their Effects

Symbolic Actions

"When people are in love, they do _____. And a person who loves another would never do _____." These kinds of unspoken expectations in your magnet are perceived as pressure by another person (see the description of a "projection" on page 52), and this pressure subconsciously makes them want to escape. As a result, you often bring about the opposite of what you want.

Symbolic Statements

Some people affirm certain ideas very frequently or early on. The more someone insists on affirming something that is not even really in question, the more they may be trying to convince themselves of it—sometimes because it doesn't exist. If someone frequently lectures you on a issue without good reason, it is often because they haven't resolved the problem for themselves yet.

Astrological Signs

As we saw in the story "Bill and the Pisces" (see page 26), excessive faith in the power of astrology—such as the belief that certain signs don't suit each other well—can also act as a magnet. While there are several basic types of people who tend to get along better or worse with each other, many other factors also play a role. Ultimately, it's about the individual person, not about the symbols associated with him or her.

Symbolic Objects

What kind of clothing does someone wear? What is his or her furniture like? What does she do for work? What kind of car does he drive? What brands does she like? These kinds of symbols can be revealing. However, people are constantly changing, and they hang on to old symbols without really thinking about it. So when you judge someone based on these symbols, keep in mind that you may be judging his or her past. The person in front of you today is not the same one you may think you are seeing. It's better to rely on your intuition instead.

 Symbolic Thoughts

There are countless mistaken ideas about love, and they program your magnetic heart with a negative force. The following are a few examples:

◆ You have to fight for love. You need to win over the other person.
◆ Love requires the extensive use of signs of affection.
◆ Time is limited. If you don't hurry and pressure the other person to make a declaration of love, you will lose him or her.
◆ It takes creativity to win someone over. Love is won only by the clever.
◆ There are rivals everywhere that need to be challenged or chased away.
◆ When things get difficult, it's because he/she can't see the truth.
◆ All the good ones are taken. If he/she is single, there must be a catch.

◆ Love exists only when you proclaim it often. If you don't say it, it's not really love.

◆ Love, pain, excitement, and drama are part of the same package. Love makes you feel butterflies in your stomach. If one of these elements is missing, it's not really love. (In reality, butterflies in your stomach represents a fear of potential loss. "Am I really loved?")

✦ Movies and Novels: Art Generates Symbols of Love

Almost every romantic comedy or drama is based upon the same basic script: Boy meets girl. Often one of them is free and willing, and the other isn't. The audience knows the two of them would be perfect together because they have so many things in common, but one of them is still hanging on to a third person or to some idea of freedom that keeps them from being together. This conflict creates intense feelings of all kinds—especially in the audience members, who are programming their own magnetic hearts in those moments when they forget that it's just fiction.

The available character must then bring the unavailable one back from the "wrong" path and convince him or her that he or she (the available one) is Mr./Ms. Right. This can all be very dramatic, and the possibility of them losing each other may be played out to almost unbearable heights. Eventually, the previously unavailable character realizes the error of his or her ways and catches the departing, hopeless suitor just in the nick of time.

These stories are wonderful, entertaining, emotional, significant, romantic, humorous...yet at the same time they create symbolic ideas about love that can also cause drama in everyday life.

Incidentally, the concept of "romantic love" is a medieval, European invention with religious origins. It took the idea of honoring an eternally unattainable divinity and transferred it onto human objects of desire. In the Romantic Era, lovesickness was elevated to an art form in literature and conversations among the educated elite. The Beloved became conceptualized as a god or goddess, a prince or princess, and the "sweet pain" of love—the delayed or thwarted satisfaction of coming together—as something to be savored.

Take a close look at the things that others are saying/thinking/doing about an issue that's important to you. Decide for yourself whether they are really true.

How to Discover and Disable Hidden Symbols

A certain experience from your past is symbolic for you. Under no circumstances do you want to live through it again, but somehow you always seem to attract similar experiences. One way to put a stop to these recurrences is by doing the following:

1. *Observe what is happening.*
2. *Look for the symbol in the situation.*
3. *Discover the pattern that this symbol represents.*
4. *Find the source of the symbol and forgive it—and yourself.*
5. *Reframe the story.*

We can see from Kathy's story below how simple and fundamentally transformative this approach can be for your magnetic heart.

How Kathy Finally Took Care of the Newspapers

Kathy is a petite, thirty-seven-year-old woman. She enjoys painting, sculpting small figurines, dancing, and expressing her feelings in a variety of ways. In the last eight years she has had three long relationships. In each case, Kathy painfully ended the relationship because her partner disrespected her and she felt used. She felt both inadequate and guilty because she couldn't figure out why things always went wrong. Kathy started searching for the pattern within her magnet:

1. *Observe what is happening: Something in my life is not right. There's something I don't want. What is it?*

Kathy's response: "There are a few specific things that I want to avoid at all costs: A man who reads the newspaper over breakfast, someone who turns on the TV as soon as he gets home, and anyone who is constantly taking off to pursue some meaningless hobby. All three of my past partners did all of these things, and it hurt me deeply."

2. *Find the symbol: Where is the symbol, and what feelings does it represent? What internal "film" have I created? Why exactly am I trying to avoid this?*

"I made a truly wonderful breakfast for the two of us, and the man who's supposed to love and cherish me hides behind his newspaper rather than noticing the meal and paying attention to me. A person

*who acts like this doesn't love or respect me. I do the housework while
he watches TV or works on his hobbies instead of talking to me when
we're together. Reading the paper and watching TV by himself are
obvious symbols of disrespect."*

  3. *Recognize the pattern: What films in your life have featured simi-
     lar symbolic actions? Was it with your first or your most recent
     partner? In your home growing up? What do these individual film
     clips have in common? These similarities are the "pattern."*

*"When I think back on it, most of my partners didn't respect me.
And they let me know this very clearly. That's the shared pattern in
these stories."*

  4. *Find the source and forgive it: Where did the pattern show up for
     the first time? Where might this film clip (the memory) have come
     from? Often it is from your childhood or a significant relationship.*

*"My father treated my mother that way. She sacrificed herself,
and he selfishly did his own thing without appreciating her. He hid
behind his newspaper as if it were a wall. And I had to watch that as
a child. It was just awful. It was then that I decided never to read the
paper when other people were around. I still don't like newspapers to
this day. And I definitely don't want to have a partner who has even
the slightest tendency to do what my father did. Unfortunately, that's
the kind of person who keeps turning up in my life."*

When Kathy realized that her father had provided the defining
film clip and was the source of her programming, she knew why her
magnet was attracting men who acted just like him. She was able to
let herself off the hook because she realized she had not done anything
wrong. She was also able to forgive her father because she recognized

that he didn't know any better. If he had been more aware of his behavior, he might have changed it.

5. Reframe the story: What might a film scene look like in which a loving person does exactly the same thing that an unloving person did before?

Kathy imagined the following story:

"I don't have a partner right now, but I imagine that he's already by my side. I can see the breakfast table in my apartment. It's Sunday morning. The previous night was wonderful, with all the love and warmth that I've always dreamed about. I can feel how much he loves me—I just know it. I go into the kitchen and make us breakfast while he is humming to himself in the shower. I love hearing that. It occurs to me to go buy some fresh bread from the shop across the street. On the way there, I pass a newspaper stand and pause for a second. I know my partner loves to read the paper—like my father used to. I buy a copy, and on the way home, I pick a few flowers from the front yard. I'm back before he gets out of the bathroom. He doesn't know I've been gone. I arrange the flowers on the table, put out the fresh bread, and place the newspaper next to his plate.

When he comes out, he stops and admires the breakfast table. I can see how happy he is. He hugs me, and we sit down.

He discovers the newspaper, looks at me, and makes some comment about how thoughtful I am—saying that he can't read the newspaper while I'm sitting there at the table. I can feel how much he loves me, and I can feel how appreciative he is about the paper. I tell him to go ahead and read it, and I ask for the travel section. We eat breakfast, enjoy the scent of the flowers, and read interesting things to each *other from our sections of the paper. I love what's taking place at my table right now."*

Another way to weaken a disruptive symbolic action in your magnet is to try to do the exact same thing that you don't like other people to do—only if it doesn't hurt anyone, of course. Try it out a few times and observe how it makes you feel. Afterward, the symbol will probably feel much less powerful, or may even disappear, because you will realize that it's just an action or an object.

How to Free Yourself from Symbolic Objects

- Sit quietly and look at the object more closely than you ever have before. Observe and feel its material and workmanship. Play around with its function, if it has one. Feel its structure and its weight. Use all of your senses to engage with the object as much as possible. Smell, feel, weigh and taste it. After a little while, it will become an object without any significance.
- Look for situations featuring a similar, but insignificant object, or one that signifies just the opposite.
- Often, the meaning of the symbol may be accurate, but can you be absolutely sure—beyond a doubt—that it's true in your case? Ask yourself this question, and feel what happens when you hear the answer.

Eric and the Tie Clip

Eric, a fifty-three-year-old salesman, had not been in a relationship since his painful split from his beloved wife seven years previously. Every morning, he tied his tie and fastened it with a golden tie clip that his wife had given him on their first anniversary. Whenever he attached the clip, he remembered the love he experienced when they were together and still felt to that day. But then he would come back to reality and would feel the emptiness in his life. The pain was so overwhelming that he couldn't face a new romance.

One day, Eric confided in a friend who told him to look at the tie clip and describe, in as much detail as possible, exactly what he was seeing: The color, the shape, the weight, the surface texture.... At that moment, Eric realized three things:

1. The pin was just a piece of metal, not his love for his wife.
2. "Worshipping" old symbols and memories wasn't a sign of love, especially not if they caused him pain.
3. There was nothing wrong with still feeling love for his ex-wife, while simultaneously meeting other women and opening himself up to them. It was neither dishonest nor a betrayal of his own sense of love. On the contrary, opening up to fulfillment and joy in his life was a sign of his love for himself.

Once he recognized this, Eric was able to throw away the symbol of his loneliness without feeling any loss.

In the following weeks, he began to sell or give away several objects from the apartment he and his ex-wife had shared. The more he did so, the freer he felt. Eric felt a near sense of elation as he got rid of first the older and then more recent objects from their shared past. He finally moved into a new apartment and completely redecorated it. Six months later, he met a new woman, and fell in love again.

Hurting yourself is not a sign of love.
A true sign of love is doing everything
you can to put a stop to your suffering.

Reframe Your Story: Love Not War!

If you experience negative emotional programs that are triggered by certain symbols, there is a wonderful way to reprogram your own magnet instantly:

Associate the past event or object with love rather than with a negative experience. Imagine the past situation during which when the symbol was used in a way that hurt you. Now ask yourself, "How could things have been different?"

Invent a new internal film featuring a person whom you love and who loves you. The person doesn't need to be real. Just imagine the perfect partner and your affection for him or her. Once you feel the corresponding emotion, imagine how this person, who loves you more than anything in the world, could use the same symbol just because he or she likes it—not knowing about your previous experiences with it. Observe this person and feel how much you love them while they are doing this. He or she is doing it because they enjoy it. It has nothing to do with you. Keep feeling your love for this person and observe what he or she does. Now feel the emotion that the old symbol is creating within you. Is it joy? Is it love?

At the moment you are able to feel this, you have freed your magnetic heart from the power of the old symbol. You won't attract this situation again in the future. And if you notice someone else doing something similar, you'll simply observe it and know deep down that it has nothing to do with you anymore.

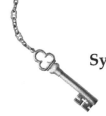

Symbols: Reason and Purpose

Reason

◆ Objects and behaviors to which you assign symbolic importance can help you make quick decisions when you find yourself in similar situations, but sometimes the decisions are made too quickly.

◆ You have associated intense feelings with symbolic objects and symbolic actions. These emotions are part of your magnet, and they attract people who are looking for the same feelings.

Purpose

◆ The purpose of uncovering every unconscious symbol that you have created is to ultimately free yourself from it. Only when you recognize an object or a memory for what it really is—a symbol of the past—can you make decisions in the present that are based on your true, current feelings.

◆ You can consciously invent new symbols for yourself and associate them with the feelings that you want to have in your magnet. These symbols will then become reminders of how you want to feel.

"It is only with the heart that one can see clearly what is essential is invisible to the eye."

Antoine de Saint-Exupéry
French author and pilot
(Quote from *The Little Prince*)
1900–1944

Putting the Fifth Secret into Practice

◆ Look for symbolic objects in your own surroundings. What do they awaken in you? If they stir unpleasant feelings like pain, loss, or sadness, use this approach to program your magnet: Try removing the objects and see how it feels. Do you have a greater sense of freedom? If so, then it's time to make some decisions.

- Are there things that cause positive feelings in you that aren't associated with any negative memories from your past? People, images, clothing, smells, sounds...? You can charge your magnet with emotions you associate with your ideal life rather than dwelling on the past.
- Observe people who seem to have a fixed attitude toward certain issues. Do they defend ideas, even when the opposite might be true? What are they trying to avoid? How do these people seem to you?

How to Reset Your Magnet

- Clear the clutter from your life. If any objects around you induce painful memories, get rid of them. If something produces both positive and negative feelings, toss it anyway. If the material value of an object prevents you from disposing of it, remember that your feelings about it are shaping your magnet and your life. Is the item worth it?
- If you find yourself strongly rejecting certain behaviors or characteristics in other people, it has something to do with you—otherwise those feelings wouldn't get activated. What is causing this and why? Does what other people do truly affect your happiness? Do you want to let other people's idiosyncrasies shape your feel-

ings and program your magnet? Or do you want to be free? It is your decision to make.

◆ What behaviors did you see in your father, mother, or an ex-partner that you have strongly rejected? In what ways do you never want to be like that or live through a similar experience again? Why? What do you think it means, and what does it symbolize? And is the meaning of the behavior true for everyone you meet? There is a strong likelihood that you will keep attracting it because of this very attitude.

The Sixth Secret

"The people around you rarely act the way you want them to, but often act the way you're afraid they will."

The Self-Fulfilling Prophecy

You are connected with others. We are all interconnected—we are social creatures. It's a law of nature. When you come into contact with other people, they can sense what you are feeling and thinking. The less they are aware of this fact, the more they will respond automatically. You have already seen for yourself how this "law of resonance" works, regardless of distance—you think about someone, and at that very moment he or she calls you. Scientists are just beginning to rediscover and explain this age-old knowledge through the concept of "morphic fields." In brief, they are starting to examine if parts of our consciousness can act as transmitters and receivers to communicate with other people.

If your actions and speech don't correspond to what you are thinking and feeling, other people will register this as dissonant and confusing—which will result in mistrust and alienation. If your thoughts, feelings, and actions match up, people will perceive you as authentic, honest, and "real." This creates trust and intimacy.

*What you say and how you want to come across
have only a small effect on your magnet.
What you are really thinking and feeling
have much stronger results.*

This is also why it's impossible to misuse the secret of your magnetic heart. Your magnetic heart is completely authentic. It projects your true feelings. If you think one thing and feel the opposite, it is what you feel that will prevail. You may wish you could direct something in a particular direction, but if your feelings contradict this, they will determine the actual path. In the short term, a person may respond to what you say. In the long term, though, she or he will sense how you feel, which will affect their subconscious responses. They may not notice that your stories and your emotions are affecting them but, sooner or later, they will follow what you are projecting as if it were their own projection.

Judith's Aversion to Liars

Judith was thirty-two when she fell in love with Harold, who was eight years older. In past relationships, Judith had had a series of experiences with men who showed remarkable similarities. In particular, they all began to lie to her at some point. The reasons were always different, but sooner or later the lies and dishonesty started appearing. For that exact reason, Judith placed an extremely high value on authenticity within herself and others. She had developed a kind of sixth sense for lies. Judith herself was compassionate, emotionally mature, and tolerant. She just couldn't handle dishonesty because she saw it as a sign of disrespect, lack of love, and immaturity.

Right from the beginning of the relationship, Harold and Judith were very open with each other. They told each other about their experiences, personal histories, hopes, dreams, and fears.

Harold quickly learned about Judith's intense dislike of being lied to, and he decided to always be truthful with her. He also knew about the secret of the self-fulfilling prophecy, and he understood that he was now subject to Judith's emotional programming. One evening, as he lay by himself in Judith's bed, Harold felt the strength of his love for her and decided to be the man who would erase all of her bad experiences with dishonesty and disrespect. He decided he would be the one to heal her wounds.

Harold made sure he was always completely open with her about his thoughts and feelings. One day he came home late, and Judith asked him where he had been. He said he had been in a café with some friends. Judith gave him an inquisitive look and responded, "Oh. Friends?"

He nodded and mentioned their names—two women and a man—and told her what the group had talked about. Harold sensed a level of mistrust that he had never felt from Judith before. As he told her about his evening, part of him started to wonder what might be making Judith suspicious. Maybe based on a past experience, she believed he had been flirtatious with other women and was afraid he would leave her? In fact, one of the two women at the table had been attractive, and Harold had flirted with her a little bit. Should he tell the jealous woman this and confirm her suspicions, even though he loved her more than anything in the world and would never dream of abandoning her?

No, he didn't want to pour any oil on the fire. After all, Harold had decided not to be one of the men who hurt her. As he talked, he noticed how uncertain he felt; the more his confusion grew, the more suspiciously Judith looked at him.

"Were the women pretty?" she asked.

He quickly shook his head no and then realized that the situation had spiraled out of his control. Completely aware of Judith's program, he was nonetheless unable to be honest with her. He realized it immediately and considered admitting to her that he hadn't told her the truth. But then he would have been validating Judith's assumption that she was always lied to. Harold realized he was caught in a trap, and he couldn't see any way out. He had become what she had feared most.

After that incident, Harold felt much worse about the relationship than before. He noticed a strange phenomenon within himself: Every time he found himself telling a lie, his desire to be completely honest diminished. Again and again, he had to fight off the feeling that Judith was trying to be lied to. Harold simultaneously felt inadequate and angry with Judith because she was putting him in such a difficult position. The relationship had suffered a distinct break, and a few months later they split up.

How Your Magnet's Field Affects Others

Imagine that you can hear other people's feelings as if they were melodies. Some pieces will sound lovely to you and produce such positive emotions that you want to hear them again and again. Some will hardly move you at all, some you may not hear consciously, and others may even make you feel bad.

As long as the beautiful melodies remain in the majority, you can handle the occasional disagreeable one. But what do you do when a melody that you find very unpleasant keeps playing loudly, over and over again?

At first you try to ignore it. You might try to learn to love it because you adore the person who is producing it. You may start thinking that love requires sacrifice. However, the jarring tune keeps playing in your head and becomes louder and louder until it eventually becomes deafening. What are you going to do?

You might try to convince the other person to play something else. You might consciously try to stop listening to it. Finally, you may even put your foot down and insist that the other person can only play the song when you're not around.

What if none of this helps? You may become angry and do everything you can to keep the other person from playing that melody. And if even that doesn't work, you will probably leave.

*Your partner, or another person
close to you, will probably act in
exactly the way you fear.
The question is not "if," but "when."*

The Truly Secret-Free Relationship

When you have a close or intimate relationship with another person, there are no real secrets. You can try to keep information to yourself, but you can't keep that person from seeing the feelings in your magnetic heart. If you believe it's best for your relationship not to say certain things, that might in fact be the case. But the other person may sense the difference between what you say and what you are thinking or feeling. As a result, you may grow apart.

Telling another person your greatest secret can be one of the greatest displays of trust, and it can create important changes in your relationship. It often takes courage, because you need to first look at the secret and avoid judging yourself for it. Only when you are able to let go of the shame or anger associated with this secret will you truly be able to tell your partner about it. One thing is certain, though: even if it seems risky, courage is ultimately always rewarded in relationships.

Every case is different, and of course you should always decide for yourself. Your magnetic heart merely helps you understand what happens between people, and it helps you understand the effects of your decision to do something or avoid doing it.

Look inside yourself, and help your partner
or loved one look inside themselves, too.
There is a lot of hurt there, so be gentle
and loving with your partner—and yourself.

Invisible Power

The less people know about the law of emotional projection and response, the more they respond automatically to the feelings of others. But what if both parties understand the secret? Does that solve the problem of the self-fulfilling prophecy? Or can one conscious partner balance out the other person's prophecy by consciously not responding to it?

What you see in an interpersonal conflict is a pattern of behavior—yours and the other person's. You might therefore try to solve the problem with a new action; for instance by trying to respond in a particular way or not at all.

However, the behavior only represents the surface, like the tip of an iceberg. It is a signpost that points to the source of the self-fulfilling prophecy within yourself or the other person. The point of origin consists of thoughts and feelings that feed the magnet, and tackling these is the only way to resolve the underlying issue.

Resolving Self-Fulfilling Prophecies

It's important to understand that the projection of any self-fulfilling prophecy has enormous power. It's time-consuming, unpleasant, and exhausting to fight it. Many people are afraid of discovering the root cause within themselves, so instead they repeatedly allow their own prophecies to be actualized. This isn't good or bad per se, but it's important to realize that this, too, is a decision.

What someone believes about you has enormous power as long as you're trying to prove that person wrong. And it loses its grip as soon as you recognize that what another person believes has little to do with you.

◆ When You Are the Source of a Self-Fulfilling Prophecy

Ask yourself what it is that you fear, and try to change the beliefs you associate with whatever it is. Your romantic partner can't do this for you—you must do it yourself. Despite what you think, things only happen if you believe they will. In order to get rid of your limiting, self-fulfilling prophecy, you must change your own internal movie (or tape). Here are two ways to do this:

1. The power of the imaginary journey

Replace your old memories and feelings with new thoughts and feelings, as demonstrated in the story about Kathy and the newspapers in the Fifth Secret (see page 88). Do this again and again, until you feel like your negative emotions about the issue have been resolved.

2. The power of truth

Evaluate whether what you think and believe are actually facts. Do the things you've experienced in the past really always hold true? Will they always happen this way without any doubt? Or could you imagine situations where everything was different? What would it be like if you found out that what you believed was wrong? How would this make you feel? For an entire week, every evening right before you go to sleep, let yourself experience these new feelings. Doing this can change the projection of your magnet!

◆ When You Are Subject to Another's Self-Fulfilling Prophecy

Your first task is to internally free yourself from the issue. If you explore your feelings, you will realize that the other person is acting as your mirror. Somewhere deep inside, you harbor the same fear that you sense in the other person. When you understand this, you hold the power to positively affect your shared relationship. Once again, you will observe how everything can change when you change yourself. If you wish—and if the other person is willing—you can watch what begins to happen together.

There is little or no chance of success if you respond to the situation on a rational level. Stop trying *not* to respond. Stop trying to prevent or prove something. Don't try to do it "well" or "right," and don't try to help "improve" the situation. All of these things will create a tangled mess that you won't be able to unravel later, and when you try to do so, you will simply reinforce the other person's undesired programming.

The programming in the other person's magnet represents strong convictions, fears, and emotional injuries. These are strong because they have been reinforced often during the person's life, and they will be able to provide a "perfect" response to any argument you might make. As long as you stay "within the game," every possible move will have been unconsciously planned out in advance. There is only one way out: Leave the playing field of argument and counterargument, action and reaction. Accepting the self-fulfilling prophecy's magnetic force is a way to begin loving yourself and to accept the other person for who they really are—without trying to change or "heal" them. Unconditional love, with no strings attached, is what will heal both of you.

"Coincidence is the pseudonym that God chooses when He wants to remain incognito."

Albert Schweitzer
Protestant theologian and pastor, organist,
music theorist, philosopher, and physician
1857–1965

The Strongest Forces Within Your Magnet

After love, fear is the strongest force in the emotional universe. If you suspect your magnet of harboring some small saboteur, it is most likely some form of fear.

We all have things that scare us, even—or especially—those of us who claim otherwise. Fear, like love and happiness, is a normal component of our emotional lives. The difference lies not in whether or not we have these feelings but in our level of awareness of them and how we deal with them. The mere mention of fear causes many people to turn away in denial. However, this challenging emotion provides a useful opportunity for growth and progress.

In our everyday lives, fear is an important automated, emotional mechanism that protects us from physical danger. In relationships, it is a perfect indicator of where our magnets harbor a charge that is causing an undesired reaction. Fear is like a finger that points to the exact cause of negative events in our lives—so that we can effect change.

Laura and the Vanishing Men

One day, Laura, a management employee at a media company, examined the similarities in her past relationships and made an astounding discovery: Almost all of the men in her life, whether the romance had lasted for weeks or years, had spontaneously left her in the end—without any apparent reason or explanation. They were suddenly just "gone." This behavior was so pronounced that Laura finally decided that she was suffering from some kind of curse. After consulting with experts on the issue and failing to see any change, Laura was ready to give up all hope for a happy, lasting relationship. To prevent these scenarios from recurring, she even started to tell prospective partners about the problem. Their response was always the same: Unbelieving astonishment and an assurance that he would never act in this way. But at some point, the same thing always ended up happening—they left without warning or explanation.

After every unsuccessful attempt to lift the apparent "curse," Laura found herself hopelessly disillusioned. She knew about the power of attraction, but she had no idea what aspect of her magnetic heart could be causing this behavior in her partners.

She remained in the dark, until one day, while talking about her childhood with a friend, she discovered the source of her projection. Laura was one of seven children in a family that was not especially well off. Out of need and desperation, her mother had sent Laura to live with relatives when she was only ten months old, and Laura stayed with them for a year-and-a-half. Even though she couldn't consciously remember it, Laura could suddenly finally connect the dots.

Her magnet had been projecting this: "A person I love deeply (mother) will spontaneously leave me (give me away) without any explanation."

That was the exact behavior that all of her previous romantic partners had demonstrated.

Even though Laura had been very young at the time of her abandonment, it didn't make a difference; the experience sparked a strong emotional response that had been stored in her subconscious. Her magnetic heart didn't care whether her experiences and the associated emotions were conscious or subconscious. The hidden fear that this early-childhood drama could be repeated was programming Laura's magnet. Sooner or later, it caused any man who spent time within range of this energy to reenact the same scenario.

Once she understood the underlying cause of her issue, Laura felt an enormous burden lift. She realized that she wasn't an inadequate person or partner. She could start to heal and reset her magnet.

First, she forgave herself because she recognized that she had never done anything wrong. Then she forgave her mother—understanding how difficult things had been and knowing that her mother had only wanted the best for her child. She was suddenly able to forgive all the men in her past who had abandoned her for no apparent reason and without explanation because she now knew the reason herself.

Our Greatest Fear*

*"Our greatest fear is not that we are inadequate,
but that we are powerful beyond measure.
It is our light, not our darkness, that frightens us.
We ask ourselves, Who am I to be brilliant,
gorgeous, handsome, talented, and fabulous?
Actually, who are you not to be? You are a child of God.
Your playing small does not serve the world.
There is nothing enlightened about shrinking
so that other people won't feel insecure around you.
We were born to make manifest the glory of God within us.
It is not just in some; it is in everyone.
And, as we let our own light shine, we consciously give
other people permission to do the same.
As we are liberated from our fear,
our presence automatically liberates others."*

Nelson Mandela
First black president of South Africa, winner of the Nobel Peace Prize

*This quotation is generally ascribed to his 1994 inaugural speech and has inspired millions of people; it is actually from the 1992 book *Return to Love: Reflections on the Principles of "A Course in Miracles"* by Marianne Williamson.

113

Self-Fulfilling Prophecies: Reason and Purpose

Reason

- All the things you have experienced and think you know about love, relationships, yourself, and other people, create emotions that program your magnet.
- These emotions are what you project to the people around you. They subconsciously, but very effectively, shape how others think about and react to you.

Purpose

- The purpose of understanding self-fulfilling prophecies is to help you recognize the enormous power and great influence that you have over the direction of your life and relationships. The more you recognize what wonderful tools your magnet and projections are, the more strength you will gather, and the more consciously you will be able to shape your present and future.
- There is a deeper purpose in recognizing who you used to be and who you are now. Uncovering and resolving your old patterns and "stories" will make you truly free to feel the beauty and intensity of new people, experiences, and adventures in the present.

Putting the Sixth Secret into Practice

◆ What fundamental attitude do you usually experience with the people you interact with regularly? Do they have a sense of trust or mistrust of others and life? How do you feel when you are within range of those two conflicting attitudes? This is how others feel about your various projections, too.

◆ Think about your relationships with people who projected their bad experiences or prejudices onto you. Were you able to escape them? Even if you loved the person very much, were you able to live with his or her mistrust in the long term? Did the relationship feel happy and easy?

◆ How do you feel when you talk to friends or acquaintances about another person? How does it feel to highlight others' positive aspects? How does it feel to judge or condemn them? Your conversation partners will respond to this pressure.

How to Reset Your Magnet

◆ What potential behavior do you fear most in other people or romantic partners? What do you believe will or could happen "sooner or later"? Is this belief really true, or is it just a figment of your imagination? Do you really want to keep programming it into your magnet just by thinking about it?

◆ Do you have strong prejudices about certain people or groups? Why is it important in your life to reject them? By doing so, you are programming a clear attraction into your magnet, and you may end up having to deal with the exact same type of person, time and again. Is it really important to your life what others think, what they do, and how they are? Isn't it much more important what *you*, yourself, do and how *you* are? Consider these questions and make clear decisions, because doing so will shape your magnet.

◆ What do you think about your own behavior? Are you "difficult" in some way? Have you been deeply hurt? Do you warn others about yourself? Are you trying to protect yourself? All of these things attract precisely what you're trying to avoid. Has being defensive ever given you the positive feelings you long for? How would it be if you could simply see, and accept, yourself as just a person with specific qualities and experiences, without any further judgment?

The Seventh Secret

"The strongest of all the forces in your magnet is your love for your own life."

Loving Yourself

Love is the strongest force in your magnet. It is the turbocharger for everything you are trying to achieve.

Almost everyone thinks they know what love is, but hardly anyone can describe it. Try it yourself: What is love? Imagine you had to explain it to a creature that had no concept of the feeling. Can you see how challenging this task is? You can describe a chair or a cup but not this sensation. You can talk about the nature of love; you can look for comparisons, or point to it through stories, as generations of artists and writers have done; or you can experience and discover what love is *not*.

This would put you on the right path to understanding love, while simultaneously revealing it within yourself. Through various experiences in our lives, we start to peel away our preconceptions about love, like peeling back the layers of an onion.

When asked how he managed to create such a perfect, lifelike lion out of a block of marble, the sculptor Michelangelo reportedly replied, "I simply remove everything that doesn't look like a lion."

Discovering love is a similar process. It's already there—you don't need to search for it. There is nothing you can do to achieve or find it. Your only task is to remove more and more of the things that are *not* love. The rest is easy.

Ask the Best Expert of All—Ask Love

If you are unsure of how to decide or behave...
If you want to transform unpleasant feelings
and thoughts...
Ask yourself one question:
"WHAT WOULD LOVE DO?"

- If a person consistently acts in a way that makes you feel bad—regardless of whether you like the person or not—ask yourself, "What would love do? Would it want me to do the same thing to myself? Would it want me to let another person treat me like that? Would love let me give myself and the other person the opportunity to create all of these negative feelings?"
- If you continually sacrifice yourself for someone because you think that is what is supposed to happen when you're in love, ask yourself: "Would love do that? Would it want me to do that to myself? Would it really want me to chase an idea of love in which affection is tied to suffering?"
- If you are constantly criticizing yourself and questioning whether you did the right thing, ask yourself: "What would love do? Would it want me to keep thinking the same pointless thoughts and hurting myself? Or would it want me to recognize that I did the best I possibly could at that particular moment—and that I learned

119

from it and am now open to experiencing new situations in my life?"

The more you let go of things that don't treat you lovingly, the more you will find and experience what you are looking for. Often, what you hold onto is exactly what holds you back.

◈ If you are considering whether it's better to act rationally and logically or to do things spontaneously and without reason—just because they are fun, ask yourself: "What would love do?"

◈ If you work at something every day that makes you feel bad and that constantly makes you feel sad and powerless, ask yourself: "What would love do? Would it want me to do that?"

◈ If you often find yourself thinking that life is hard and you're much less happy than other people, ask yourself: "What would love do? Would it want me to think those things about myself and the gift of my life?"

Gabriela's Body

Gabriela is a wonderful woman in her mid-forties. Whenever she enters a room, she inspires feelings of joy, affection, and security within the people around her. Everyone who gets to know her is enchanted by her face, attitude, and gentle, understanding way with people. It's almost impossible to imagine having an argument with this warm woman. And yet Gabriela was physically abused by both of her last partners. How can a person who has such a strong sense of caring, compassion, and acceptance in her magnet attract these kinds of negative mates?

After Gabriela learned about the magnetic heart and its effects, she decided to get to the bottom of her issue. She decided there could only be one reason why aggressors felt drawn to her: They saw her as a victim. She searched for the problem in her magnet that could be creating her sense of powerlessness, and she quickly found it: She felt like a victim of her own body.

Gabriela was a little heavier than average, something that everyone who met her found harmonious and beautiful because her physique seemed to match her nurturing personality perfectly. In the eyes of others, her fashion sense and makeup only highlighted her beauty.

However, Gabriela didn't like the way she looked. She rejected her body as being too fat, and felt unable to lose weight. She saw her body as a burden that prevented her from attracting "good" men. She believed that with her appearance, it was only natural to attract men who would ultimately reject her, just as she rejected herself.

In fact, that's exactly what always happened. Gabriela was punishing herself for her body, and she found men who did the same. When she recognized the results of her self-disgust, she made an extremely powerful and heartfelt decision: Never again would a man hit her or treat her badly. She realized that it was completely crazy to think she could reject herself and then hope that a man wouldn't do the same.

When Gabriela discovered that her rejection of herself was creating just the opposite of what she actually desired, she started to look at her body in the same positive way that her friends and acquaintances had been doing for years: As a wonderful body that reflected the love she felt for others. Gabriela began to feel love for herself. From that point on, she attracted men who recognized her beauty and loved her exactly as she was. Surprisingly, she began to lose weight slowly but steadily—without even trying! Her need to overeat, and her longing for self-acceptance, had simply disappeared.

Why It's So Important to Love Yourself: An Example

Let's assume a person has tended to be a victim throughout his or her life. The individual's parents, partners, and life in general have rarely treated him or her very well. The person in question is not at fault here, but these observations and experiences have created a sense of powerlessness within them. Their internal, emotional film attracts the following types of people who, for one reason or another, find this type of feeling attractive:

1. Aggressors...

...because they can sense an easy target. Aggressors tend to be lazy. They follow the path of least resistance, and the weakest target becomes their plaything. If the target discovers their strength, the aggressor will likely leave and hunt for a new weak target.

2. Other victims...

...because they feel understood and safe. We are all looking for love, and being understood gives us a sense of intimacy.

3. "Enablers" and comforters...

...in other words, the kind of people who feel better when they see how badly the victim is doing or who get most of their self-worth by feeling they are helping others. Enablers depend on people who aren't doing well—otherwise they would be out of work. Some are really well intentioned, but others get a sense of superiority or even happiness; for example, "When I see how poorly X is doing, it makes me feel better about my lesser problems."

None of these people can really help the victim escape this role. As soon as the victim recognizes the root cause of the attraction within his or her own magnet, however, he or she becomes an observer. And once he or she figures out how to stop feeding or empowering the root cause within their own magnet, they are transformed into a strong decision-maker. Loving yourself and your own life is the key to this transformation.

As I Began to Love Myself *

As I began to love myself I found that anguish and
emotional suffering are only warning signs that I was living
against my own truth. Today, I know this is
AUTHENTICITY.

As I began to love myself I understood how much it can offend
somebody as I try to force my desires on this person,
even though I knew the time was not right and the person
was not ready for it, and even though this person was me.
Today I call it
RESPECT.

As I began to love myself I stopped craving for a different life,
and I could see that everything that surrounded me
was inviting me to grow. Today I call it
MATURITY.

As I began to love myself I understood that at any circumstance,
I am in the right place at the right time, and everything happens
at the exactly right moment. So I could be calm. Today I call it
SELF-CONFIDENCE.

* The source of the quote is unclear; some cite Kim and Alison McMillen's 2001 book *When I Loved Myself Enough*, though the book's version is different from what is written here. Others claim that Chaplin read this version of "As I Began to Love Myself" aloud at the celebration of his 70th birthday on April 16, 1959.

As I began to love myself I quit stealing my own time,
and I stopped designing huge projects for the future.
Today, I only do what brings me joy and happiness, things I love
to do and that make my heart cheer, and I do them in my own
way and in my own rhythm. Today I call it
SIMPLICITY.

As I began to love myself I freed myself of anything that is no
good for my health—food, people, things, situations, and every-
thing that drew me down and away from myself. At first I called
this attitude a healthy egoism. Today I know it is
LOVE OF ONESELF.

As I began to love myself I quit trying to always be right,
and ever since I was wrong less of the time.
Today I discovered that is
MODESTY.

As I began to love myself I refused to go on living in the past
and worry about the future. Now I only live for the moment,
where EVERYTHING is happening. Today I live each day,
day by day, and I call it
FULFILLMENT.

125

*As I began to love myself I recognized that my mind
can disturb me and it can make me sick. But As I connected
it to my heart, my mind became a valuable ally.
Today I call this connection
WISDOM OF THE HEART.*

*We no longer need to fear arguments, confrontations,
or any kind of problems with ourselves or others.
Even stars collide, and out of their crashing new worlds
are born. Today I know
THAT IS LIFE!*

Charles Chaplin
Director, actor, comedian, and composer
1889–1977

The Trap: Trying to Love Yourself

Challenging yourself to "love yourself" can be very powerful. If it works for you, keep this wonderful phrase in your heart and feel its fulfilling effects.

If you have trouble with it, you may be caught in the "self-love trap": However hard you try, the feeling keeps escaping you. Eventually, you may feel you cannot do it. It's almost as if the more you want it, the more it eludes you. Loving yourself seems to be something that you can spend your whole life trying to accomplish. However great all of these suggestions may sound, ultimately you're left with the feeling that it's not really working the way it should.

Why is it so hard to feel love for yourself? Because, strictly speaking, it's impossible to "love yourself." It's a trap!

❧ "Love yourself!" is a challenge to do something. But you can't do anything to create love. It's impossible to love yourself if the love isn't already there. It's as if someone were to tell you, "Love that person over there." It won't happen just because you want it to.

❧ "Love yourself!" is an instruction for your rational mind. But your mind can't love anything, let alone itself. Love is an internal state—like peace—that goes beyond logical thought. If you wanted to assign a physical location to love, it is usually felt in and around the heart.

❧ "Love yourself!" is a narrative that suggests there's something wrong with you because you clearly don't love yourself enough. But when you feel like there's something wrong with you, that emotion or thought blocks feelings of love.

◆ "Love yourself!" can also cause the exact opposite to happen. When you find that it's not working, your feelings of inadequacy, self-rejection, and doubt grow even stronger and the thought "I just can't manage to love myself" keeps surfacing.

Fortunately, there is a solution: Reframe it! As a playful experiment, take a moment to imagine what it would be like if you didn't have to love yourself at all. Then evaluate how it would feel.

Do you feel something?

At the very moment you stop trying to love yourself and simply recognize that you as a person are doing your very best—when you realize what it means to be human with all your strengths and weaknesses, successes and failures—that's when you will feel love for your life and accept it as a gift. The more this unintentional type of love shapes your magnet, the more you will experience your life as a series of unending miracles and gifts.

*When you stop believing in the narrative
that you need to love yourself, you give yourself
a wondrous gift: You are free to realize
that you already do!*

How "Loving Your Life" Affects Your Magnet

If it has been hard for you to love yourself in the past, try loving your life instead (see the exercise below).

- If you love your life more than anything, you will stop hurting yourself and letting others hurt you. People will keep saying the same things they always have, but you will stop arguing with them—because whenever you do, you lose a battle that isn't yours to fight. As you come to learn more about the secret of your magnetic heart, you will start to understand why people act the way they do. You will stand up and say whatever it is you need to say, and you will start acting out of love for yourself, rather than struggling against someone or something.

- You will become less judgmental because you'll sense that it's not good for you. The more you feel this kind of love within yourself, the less your magnet will attract those seeking to take advantage of you, and the less vulnerable you will become.

- If you love and appreciate your life as a gift, your magnet will project this. Unhealthy or weak individuals, who up until now have been dependent upon you, or have demanded a great deal from you, will sense that you are no longer doing things to hurt yourself. Because it feels great to spend time with someone who loves his or her life and refuses to hurt him- or herself, the people

129

around you will be reminded that they can also do the same for themselves.

*Love is understanding and compassion.
The more you understand yourself
and others the more you will be able
to accept things as they are, and the more
love you will feel within.*

Someone who condemns you and others is unhealthy. Someone who blames the world is unhealthy. Someone who wants you to be something you are not is unhealthy. This is because they are hurting themselves with every thought, and no healthy person would do that voluntarily. If you are able to understand why people act this way—because elements within their magnets force them to produce these responses—you will stop supporting their illness. You will respond less, which will help keep their problem from spreading to you.

"If you want to be loved, then love!"

Lucius Annaeus Seneca
Roman philosopher, playwright, natural scientist, and statesman
4–65 AD

Three Simple Exercises
to Help You Love Your Life More

**"People Who Have Me in Their Lives Are Lucky.
Why?"**

The more answers you can find to this question, the more open you will become to loving yourself. Remember: Love doesn't mean "doing" something. The goal is to recognize who and what you "are," as well as how valuable each of your wonderful qualities is. The more you understand your value, the more others will recognize it too. Explore your endearing qualities, starting every sentence with "I am..."

131

"Am I Loving Myself When...?"

If you don't feel good, regardless of the reason, there is often a vague feeling that you need to do something or make some kind of change. At the same time, you don't feel good about just any kind of response or change. Maybe the feeling you're really looking for is simply inner peace?

In difficult situations, ask yourself: "Am I loving myself when I do this? What would be the loving thing to do right now?"

Check every thought that comes to mind by asking this question, and notice what happens inside you.

Expect a Miracle and a Gift!

The following extremely effective exercise will program your magnet to "love your own life."

Before you go to sleep each night, look back at your day and ask yourself: "What was the gift I received today? What was the miracle I experienced today?" You will always be able to find at least one of each, because it's your job to create their definition. You don't need to justify yourself to anyone.

In the morning before you get out of bed, take a moment to remember your previous day's miracle and gift. If you wish, give thanks for them. You'll learn to recognize what you do have, instead of focusing energy on what is missing.

Observe how your day, the people around you, and the events you experience change after you have been doing this exercise for a while.

Incidentally, never force yourself to do an exercise—that's a waste of time. Only do it if it creates a sense of curiosity and joy within you. The feeling of joy is our most important signpost in life, our most valuable personal advisor. Whatever brings you this positive feeling is the right thing. The goal is always to sift through the endless puzzle pieces to find the one that completes your own picture. It's a game—just play!

Loving your own life starts with the decision to take risks, relinquish control— no matter what. After that, step back and watch the miracle happen.

What Will Change When You Love Your Life More?

- Several conflicts will disappear, or become easier to solve, because you no longer demand love, recognition, or appreciation.
- You will attract more and more people who feel good in your presence.
- You will deter people who can't handle the fact that you are inwardly independent and free.
- You will blame others less because you blame yourself less.
- You will project a sense of trust because you trust yourself. Others will change their attitude toward you for the better.
- You will reduce the number of automatic responses and counter-responses from the people around you.
- You can react to others, but you don't always feel the need to.
- You no longer want to be "nice" and "good" so that people will like you—but you will still do good things out of love.
- You will spend less time chasing after reward and recognition.
- You won't let yourself be used anymore.

◆ You will be able to give without expecting something in return.

◆ You will be able to simply do nothing, without feeling guilty.

◆ You will allow yourself to be touched by something because you will know it comes without any obligation.

◆ In many cases, your allergies, psychosomatic illnesses, and physical ailments will disappear or improve. What remains will meet with less internal rejection.

◆ You will do things that fulfill you, and will receive even more in return.

◆ People who used to worry about you will have one less thing to worry about.

◆ People who used to be dependent upon you will be freed because you are able to resolve your mutual codependency through your love for yourself. This doesn't mean you are abandoning the other person. In fact, you'll probably be even closer than before because you no longer feel obligated to be together. And if you feel like leaving is the right thing to do, then do it. In that case, it's the right thing for the other person, too.

◆ People who have lost their love for themselves may rediscover it because the projection of love from your magnet is transferred to the people around you (remember the mirror neurons discussed on page 76). Through the law of resonance, your love will draw out love in others. And if the other person isn't ready for it yet, your own magnetic field of love for yourself will create a protective cloak around you.

And all of this will occur without any planning or effort! Loving your own life is the greatest present you can give yourself and others. As seen above, there are a huge number of positive reasons to put yourself first. All it takes is a decision on your part: Deciding to experience what happens if you dare to try.

Love Is Often Misunderstood

- Where in the universe is it written that love means putting up with, and suffering from, other people's behavior? Yes, love means letting another person be him- or herself; but it also means valuing the gift of your own life so highly that you don't repress your spirit.

- Where is it written that you aren't allowed to hurt other people with the decisions you make for yourself? If a certain situation causes you pain, it's a mark of love to take action and end your suffering. Torturing yourself is not a sign of love, and it is never rewarded, even if generations of mothers and fathers have told their children that it is. Deciding for yourself and your own life's happiness is the responsible thing to do.

- Where is it written that love means taking responsibility for another person's happiness and satisfaction? The moment you believe you are responsible for another person's happiness, you abandon love for your own life. Others may feel joy when you are there. But there are many sources of happiness, and if you

135

were to vanish from the world tomorrow, their life would still go on.

 Is it true that love means not making any demands? That's one of the greatest conflicts in our understanding of love. It's true, love itself makes no demands, and being human means having needs, hopes, and desires. But if you love yourself for who you are, you will allow the other person to find his or her own fulfillment.

A Short Detour: Everything Is Easier Without Guilt

There's one word that has an enormous impact on both you and your magnet: guilt! When you feel guilt, regardless of whether it's toward yourself or someone else, you make yourself a victim. You become dependent on forgiveness, on making things right, on other people's opinions. Your magnet will project these feelings outward, and it will attract people who want to play the guilt-victim game with you.

 *The Experiment*

At an elementary school, a few teachers tried an experiment. They told the children that they were going to play a special game that involved removing a bad word—"guilt"—from their minds. The children played along enthusiastically. Afterward, one mother reported, "When my daughter Lisa came home, I asked her what she had done in school today. She said, 'We threw a bad word out of our heads.' I asked her what the word was. Lisa thought for a minute, then grinned at me and said, 'I forget.'"

There is no such thing as guilt in the universe. There is only cause and effect. When something happens, it causes something else to happen. When someone does something, there is an effect, and someone else reacts.

Guilt is a feeling, not a fact. It is something that human beings invented in order to make quicker decisions or judgments, to set up rules for living together, and especially to gain power over others. It isn't beneficial to program your magnet with this negative emotion.

Like everything else, the idea of "guiltlessness" can be easily misunderstood. People naturally do things that have negative effects on others. The point is not to gloss over this or to justify unethical or inconsiderate behavior. It is simply to take away the negative impact that is exerted on your magnet by a word with centuries of baggage.

The easiest, most effective way to do this is to treat it like the children did in their game. Replace "guilt" with the word "cause." That's the only thing you need to change. It's just a tiny thought process, but it will have an enormous impact on your life. Try it and see what feels freer and easier for you:

"My father is guilty of _____ because he always _____."

or

"My father often did _____, and sometimes he did _____. I watched him, and I became convinced it was wrong. This conviction is now part of my magnet, and it's attracting the following kinds of people into my life…"

You may gain a new perspective on incidents where you inadvertently caused something to happen. For instance:

"I did or said something that had a negative impact on another person. It wasn't my intention.

I will tell the person that, and I might do something to make up for it."

Whether or not the person accepts your offer and how he or she responds to it is no longer in your hands. Do what you think is appropriate. You can only present some way of trying to make up for the incident—whether or not the other person accepts it is not your responsibility.

Yes, you can feel sorry about something. Yes, you can learn from it. Yes, you can make up for something if it feels right to do so. Yes, you can tell the other person that you're sorry for what you said or did. But that's where your role ends. You are free. If they want to suffer by continuing to judge you, that is their decision, not yours. Your job is not to force someone to forgive you. Forgiveness is a free—and very personal—decision made by every individual.

Guilt is a feeling, not a fact. A victim thinks about guilt and feels a heavy burden. A conscious, aware, and empowered person thinks about cause and effect, and senses the right path.

- Feelings of guilt use up energy, create a feeling of dependency (on the other person's goodwill), and dampen your mood.
- Thinking about the cause channels your energy into change—it creates recognition and growth, and produces a positive attitude toward yourself.

Loving Yourself: Reason and Purpose

Reason

◆ One good reason for loving your life is the knowledge that it activates the strongest possible force in your magnetic heart for creating an even more fulfilling life.

◆ The call to "love yourself" often creates pressure that makes it even more difficult to love your life. That's because love is not an activity, nor can it be set as a goal to be achieved through taking certain actions. It's not possible for your rational mind to love yourself, because logic cannot love.

Purpose

◆ The purpose of loving yourself and your own life is to recognize that you already have what you are really seeking—both within and around you. Understanding this will help you peel away the layers of fear and other negative emotions that you harbor, making love the strongest force in your magnet.

◆ Loving yourself and your own life is not a goal to be achieved. It's a way to get closer to understanding yourself and others.

Putting the Seventh Secret into Practice

◆ Look at your own life: When were you the happiest? Did some of those times include moments when you were alone? Is another person really necessary in order for you to feel love toward your own life?

◆ Observe how people respond to you when you feel happy. That's the effect of your magnetic heart! Consciously experience how your world changes when you let love flow in and out.

◆ Pay attention to the people who tell you that you should love yourself more. Do they love themselves? Look at others whose lives are in flux: Are they thinking about how to love themselves, or do they talk about it often?

◆ Watch friends and acquaintances who are in romantic relationships. After the honeymoon stage, are they really much happier and more fulfilled than before? Does a relationship guarantee fulfillment and happiness?

How to Reset Your Magnet

◆ What thoughts and experiences are preventing you from feeling love for yourself or your life? Don't let these thoughts remain in your head for long or they will unintentionally start to affect your magnet. Write them down. These ideas only survive because they are unseen and unexamined. Once you have jotted everything down, check each and every statement to see if it's true. For each one, find up to three examples that demonstrate the opposite.

◆ Whenever possible, make sure that your emotional "accounts" are balanced. If you feel guilt toward someone for something, recognize that there is no such thing as guilt—only imbalance. Think about what could balance it out, and then do it. That is the end of your role. If the person has died or is no longer able to be reached, do the same thing for another person instead. Once you have done this, it will feel like the case is closed and you are inwardly free.

◆ Discover what makes you a lovable person, regardless of what you do for others. Don't ask, "What am I doing?" Instead ask, "What am I like?"

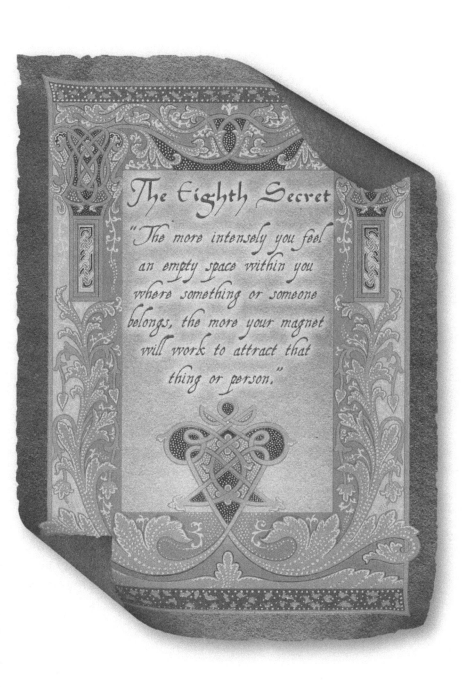

The Eighth Secret

"The more intensely you feel an empty space within you where something or someone belongs, the more your magnet will work to attract that thing or person."

Your Inner Room

*Your Inner Room is the place within you
that is designed for an object or person
(and resulting feeling) of your longing.
Whenever you let yourself sense it,
you are activating your magnet so that it can
attract the object or person even more forcefully.*

Your magnet will increasingly attract people and events as you begin to picture your goal with more intensity. However, not everyone has such a creative imagination; it also takes discipline and a good deal of persistence once your initial enthusiasm has worn off.

The secret of your Inner Room is just as powerful—if not more so—as when you imagine a goal and feel like you are on the path toward it. When you work with the power of your Inner Room, you don't actively create your goal. Instead, you use the energy from an already existing feeling—a feeling that something is missing—and transform it into a positive magnetic attraction.

How to Discover Your Inner Room

Whenever you feel an unrequited longing for something, picture it in your mind. Instead of trying to imagine that you already have it—which many people have trouble doing in the long term—guide the picture further, toward the space within you where it will end up when you do have it. This place is the source of your longing.

Many people don't want to explore their Inner Room because they are afraid of experiencing a lack of fulfillment and emptiness there. They think, "An empty room inside me filled with a great longing... how depressing! I don't want to feel that."

However, this place and these feelings are already a part of you. It is there and it affects you, regardless of whether you want it to or not. You have two options:

1. *You can continue to think that you have this depressing, empty room within you, and you can avoid looking at it—for instance, by repressing your longings, distracting yourself each time the issue comes up, or trying to think positive thoughts.*

There's nothing wrong with any of these solutions as long as you still feel you are attracting what you deeply desire into your life. If not, then you will feel your Inner Room is a void, representing a lack of what you really want. This will only attract an even greater lack of this particular longing in your life.

2. *The second option is to see your Inner Room as preparation for the inevitable fulfillment of your longing, not as a lack of something. And when it arrives, it will fit perfectly into the space you've prepared!*

What You Will Experience When You Find Your Inner Room
If you look within yourself for the source of your longing, the image of your room will develop all by itself. You might not visualize it but simply feel it. That's fine—it's your own personal experience.

You may discover all kinds of feelings in the room. The less pleasant ones are the reason your longing hasn't been attained yet. Simultaneously, something unexpected will probably happen: You will enjoy discovering what has been blocking your fulfillment. It is one of the nicest experiences you can have, because it's the truth. You see the truth within yourself. You will finally recognize what has been programming your magnet to prevent your happiness and you will feel a deep sense of gratitude. Additionally, once you uncover and truly understand your unpleasant feelings, they lose their reason for being—to alert you to their existence so you can start to create change. When they are no longer needed, they simply vanish. At that moment, an enormous internal healing process will have begun.

Above all, you may also find joy in this room—an anticipatory joy about what is going to come into your life.

How to Activate
the Power of Your Inner Room

Step 1

You would like to have something because you can tell that it is missing in your life. This is a fundamental power that is already working
within you, without you having to do anything. As long as you only
sense that it is absent, you will feel a lack; this feeling in your magnet
will cause you to keep missing whatever it is you long for. Energy
is never lost in the universe, not even the energy of your unfulfilled
desires. If nothing changes for a while—either because you're suppressing your longing or because your actions are unsuccessful—the
power won't be able to flow outward; instead, it will turn inwardly
against you. This "powerlessness" can lead to feelings of dissatisfaction, depression, restlessness, sadness, anger, and resignation, which
can eventually lead to internal and external illness. It's not a faulty
design—it's supposed to force us to make changes so that we can come
closer to the individual purpose of our existence!

Once you understand this, you will no longer be resigned or angry
when you sense that something is missing. Instead, you'll realize that
the point of dissatisfaction is to create momentum for change, and
you will start to take advantage of it.

Step 2

Now imagine a room deep within you, where whatever it is that you are missing belongs. This place is simply waiting—completely empty. The emptiness acts like a vacuum, attracting exactly what you are lacking. It could look like an actual room, or it could simply be a feeling of dark emptiness, with a strong force of attraction—pulling something toward you. Use whatever works best for you and your imagination.

Step 3

Whenever thoughts and feelings arise about the things you're lacking, bring your consciousness back to your Inner Room: Invite the missing thing to come into the room. Feel that the room is pulling it in because that's exactly where it belongs.

Do you feel a sense of relief when you associate a sense of longing with the image of the Inner Room you have prepared for it? You might find that an idea that once caused you feelings of inadequacy now brings you joy. Whenever you feel like something is missing, simply feel it being attracted to you. That's all you need to do in order to reset your magnet.

Connie and the Unavailable Men

For more than four years, Connie tried very hard to find the right romantic partner. In addition to the usual approaches—like going to parties and other events—she also used a large online dating service. Connie is an attractive woman in her late twenties so she and her friends were equally confused as to why she couldn't find a good man among all of the people she met.

Again and again, her magnet attracted guys who declared their love for her on the first or second date and started making plans for the future. In many cases, Connie let it happen to "give the relationship a chance," as she put it. Every time, it ended painfully—sometimes quickly, sometimes after a few weeks or months. The reasons for each failure seemed to be different, though the results were always the same: The men were married, living in another country or far away, overburdened with children and an ex-wife, still dealing with the pain of past relationships, drowning in work, and/or just looking for a brief fling.

Connie suffered so greatly from her failures that it started to affect her career and her physical well-being. No matter what kind of advice her friends gave her, it didn't seem to change her bad luck with relationships. What was the common thread? What was the source in Connie's magnetic heart that continually attracted these situations?

While her partners were very different, they did have one thing in common—not one of them was really "available." When Connie

149

realized this, she searched her magnetic heart for a conviction or a feeling that might be attracting "unavailable" men. She found the cause when a friend helped her take an honest look at her own feelings, and Connie finally admitted to herself that she wasn't truly available either. She wanted a relationship like those in the romance novels she enjoyed reading, but at the same time, she was afraid of a binding partnership that might even involve living together. Connie was afraid of losing her freedom.

For the first time, Connie understood that she did not have an Inner Room that was prepared for a long-term relationship. She admitted that she loved the excitement of new adventures, and that she saw fear and hope as an important part of romance. Because of the books and movies she liked to read and watch, Connie was completely convinced that the protagonists emotional drama was not only normal, but was actually proof of their love for each other. That's exactly what she had experienced in her relationships so far. The only man in her life with whom she had a relationship that felt familiar, physically satisfying, and peaceful—an on-again-off-again situation that had lasted for years—seemed "too boring" to her.

As soon as Connie admitted this to herself, she stopped suffering. She now knew that she was creating these types of relationships, and that she had the ability to change them at any time. She stopped feeling like a victim, and her strength returned. Connie decided to slow down her constant search for a man, and spent the extra time focusing on her existing friendships. One of these friends was the man she had long ago dismissed as too dull.

She discovered that he could be not just a friend and an occasional fling, but also a valuable partner—and they began the deepest relationship she had ever experienced.

Preparing Your Inner Room for a Life Partner
Imagine that over the course of your life, you have had a room inside you that was intended for a particular person. Go ahead and imagine it as a real room in the house of your life, one in which previous partners have lived.

Does this room even exist right now? Is it stable, or does it come and go?
Go into your "partner room" and look around. Do you encounter painful memories? Is there still someone living in it, even if that person isn't in your life anymore? Is there an altar with pictures of people you have lost, or other remnants of a relationship? Are there signs on the wall listing your expectations and rules for future residents? Are you ready to let the next tenant change everything in the room? Could he or she completely redecorate it?

Are you really free?
If not, for your own sake you need to make more space. If you want someone to come into your life and/or to feel more comfortable with you, that person will need room to do it. You should actively create this area and clear it out. Just wishing is not enough—that's like

wanting something without giving anything in return. Only when you actually have an empty room in your life can you invite a guest to stay and feel at home. The person you are longing for may just want to stay awhile.

Your Decision Is the Key

When someone comes along who wants to share your "room," you have to decide to change your life so that you project that you are truly available for a real partner. If you are ready for anything to happen as a result of your shared love, you are opening the gates to heaven. Trying to "protect" your life, or large parts of it, from change leaves less space for new, positive things. As a result, you will keep reliving your past in the present, and on into the future.

Your Priorities Determine the
Type of Relationship You Will Have

Let's say that a romantic relationship is the fifth most important thing in your life right now, after your career, hobby, sports, and certain friends. You will most likely attract potential partners who feel the same way: You will occupy the same position in their lives.

In the course of the relationship, you might feel much more for the person than you expected, and your partner might move up to first or second place in your life. Naturally, you would hope that your ranking changes in your partner's life too. If it doesn't, then you have a problem.

You can avoid this situation by understanding the significance of the Inner Room when it comes to the relationships in your life, by understanding your priorities and understanding that other people might have different priorities, then calibrating your relationship choices accordingly.

The following exercise will help: In no particular order, write down all of your dreams that are important to you in different areas of your life. Next, arrange them in order of priority—what is in first/second/third place, etc.? Or, if it makes more sense, what would be the easiest/second-easiest, etc. to give up?

The results might surprise you.

Now that you know about the secret of your Inner Room, it will be much easier for you to understand the people you get involved with. You will also be more quickly able to recognize which relationships have potential, and which don't.

Your Inner Room: Reason and Purpose

Reason

◆ Everything that happens in your life requires your time and attention, including an Inner and Outer Room.

◆ Your Inner Room is the sense that you have space for a longed-for person, situation, emotion, or object. It is the feeling of wanting to change your life when the object of your desire comes along. It is not an absence but a sense of fulfillment. You can already feel what is coming, and you have the room ready for it. It's an invitation for another person or situation to have a place in your life and heart.

◆ You will be able to tell how much you or someone else really wants something based on the space that you and/or the other person make available for it.

Purpose

◆ The purpose of your Inner Room has to do with loving yourself. As long as you hold on to the past, to illusions, or to insignificant things, new things cannot really take hold. Letting go means loving yourself because you are giving yourself and your life the freedom to accept the new gifts that are coming your way.

Putting the Eighth Secret into Practice

- Observe, and ask yourself: When people wish really hard for something and don't get it, were they truly ready for it? Are they really flexible? Would they be willing to change their lives for it? Or are they actually afraid of experiencing or reliving/repeating something unpleasant? Is it possible that they are actually using their lack of something to gain attention?

- If you want the new object of your longing to come to you, you will need to let go of something old, either inwardly or outwardly. Maybe it's your belief that you have already experienced the best thing out there. Or the concept that only such-and-such a thing would be perfect. What is this old idea in your life? Do you love yourself enough to create the space for a fulfilling future?

- Observe people whose lives are full of positive new things. What do they have in common? How do they respond to surprising changes or deviations from the plan? How easy is it for them to build a room where fresh opportunities can unfold? Do they hold on to decisions and opinions once they've been formed, or do they have a flexible opinion about what is "right"?

How to Reset Your Magnet

◆ Create a unified vision of everything that belongs in your life. Don't limit yourself to an image of a partner who acts in a particular way. Give your longings plenty of room. Ideally, you should visualize a "way of being." Don't cast any real people or figures with any specific physical characteristics in this internal film—just see how it feels when you watch the clip.

◆ If it is a true, deep longing, what you are longing for already belongs to you. It awaits you somewhere along your life path. Imagine a room or a feeling of magnetism that will attract exactly that which belongs to you. You won't get what you "want to have," you'll get something that "belongs with you" or is "already coming to you."

◆ Whenever you discover that you are missing something, you won't feel a sense of absence, but rather the presence of an Inner Room that is intended for it within you.

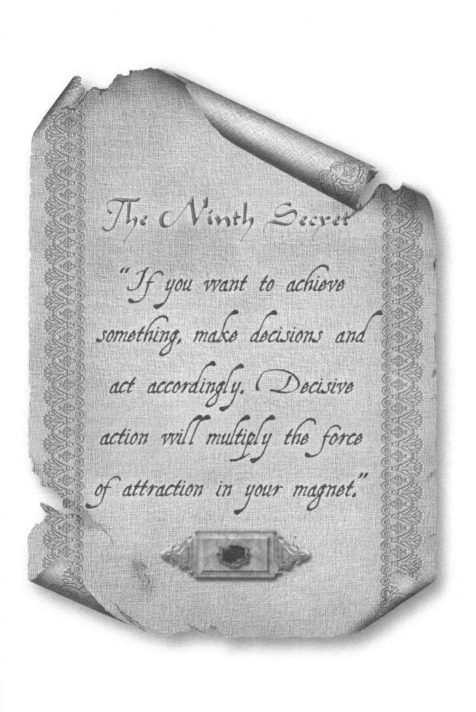

The Ninth Secret

"If you want to achieve something, make decisions and act accordingly. Decisive action will multiply the force of attraction in your magnet."

Decision and Action

In some situations, you know where you want to go but not exactly how to get there. Because of your uncertainty, you often don't go anywhere at all.

The more you utilize the power of your magnet and experience its effects, the more clearly you will understand that it's not important whether a particular action or path will ultimately lead to success. The important thing that allows the attractive power of your magnet to work is that you act as soon as you sense what it is that you want.

In taking action, you are drawing attention to what you want in your life. You are putting your wishes out "on the market" so that they can be brought to fulfillment.

Once you create a tangible feeling of action surrounding your wish, you begin to make it reality.

Do that which you want to have happen!
Start to act as though it has already
been promised to you, and you will
start to experience it. The universe
loves when you take action,
and it responds accordingly.

"It is not enough to have knowledge; one must also apply it. It is not enough to want; one must also do."

Johann Wolfgang von Goethe
German poet
1749–1832

Even if the force of your magnet is already working on its own, your actions will set additional positive energy in motion around the issue in question:

◆ Clarity: Your actions will show you and others that you have made a decision.
◆ Power: Your actions will show you and others that, when it comes to this issue, you are not a victim but are in charge of your life.
◆ Confidence: Your actions contribute believability to your clarity, increasing your faith in yourself and your own strength.

◆ Opportunity: Your actions are a practical way of opening doors, so that things can come to you. Sometimes, instead of letting in your desired goal, the door lets in a person who opens another door for you.

Uncertain? Act Anyway!
It's easy to take action, even from a position of uncertainty. Often it's enough just to take the first few steps. This will activate forces in your magnet that will amaze you later on.

◆ If you want a new apartment but don't have the money for it yet, look anyway. Read ads, look at places, and feel what it's like to know that you'll be renting a new place soon.
◆ If you long for a partner, don't stop at simply longing and imagining, or you will start to feel a lack. Do something. Take advantage of your friends and other contacts—but keep in mind that the changes may be small and not every effort will yield results.
◆ If you're looking for a new job, imagine yourself pouring the projections from your magnet—everything that you really are—into your application before you send it off. Then, imagine how it will affect the recipients, ensuring that they appreciate the real you.
◆ If you have an interview or another important meeting coming up, take a moment the night before to imagine that your magnetic heart is in the room with you during the meeting. Imagine it lying on the table between you and your conversation partner, exerting

its force. You don't know the specifics of the room or the other person, but it doesn't matter. Just imagine it. The next day, you will go into the meeting knowing that your magnet has been lying there since the previous evening, doing its work.

How to Activate Dynamic Action

1. Become a "Decision-Maker"

First, make a decision: Do you really want to be open to new things? Are you ready for anything to happen? Are you prepared to experience the adventure that will take place in some part of your life—or your entire life—if you simply stop living out your past? Or if you stop reliving your parents' story or trying to be their opposite?

It will certainly be exciting, because there's no way of knowing what will happen. Still, you can be sure that it will be new, inspiring, and interesting.

If you feel the answer spontaneously, great! If you're more the type to think things through, that's fine too. Give yourself time. Mull it over, and above all—feel it! The answer to whether you are really open and available to new situations will not come from your head. It will come from your heart. It's a fundamental question—and the answer will change your life!

*Make a decision. It will give your life momentum,
and it will charge your magnet with your desire
for change. If you don't make a decision,
a decision will be made for you.*

You're always making decisions. Even if you think you don't have any control over a particular situation and avoid making a decision, you are still making a choice: You're deciding to be inactive.

Don't be afraid of making the "wrong" decision. There's no such thing. There are only decisions and results, and then new decisions and different results.

2. Free Yourself from Old Burdens

Once you have made a decision, you set the universe in motion with your action! As you have already learned, the past can block your magnet—so here are a few tried-and-true suggestions for freeing yourself from the past. Test them out and see what works for you.

◆ Make sure that past relationships are really over. It's important to do this in a way that creates a feeling of love within you. Finding closure doesn't always mean breaking off contact. It means reaching an internal state that doesn't cause you any more pain. Is there something else that you need to say? Say it. Write a letter or an email. It doesn't matter how long ago it was, or if or how the other person responds. You are doing it for yourself, not for anyone else.

162

◆ Feel what it's like to let go of images that keep bringing your past to the present. Some people practically archive their past experiences. This is not good or bad, it just depends on what kind of feelings it creates within you. If it's too big of a step, start with one image and see what happens when you let go of it.

◆ Look at your personal contacts. Which relationships are holding steady, and which ones are developing? Where are people coming together to primarily reminisce about days gone by, and who gives you a sense of forward movement? Where are new things being created? Maybe you'd like to see how it feels to spend your time differently?

◆ Look for opportunities to experience new perspectives on life. If your free time is limited, see what it would be like to shift your focus a little—maybe away from entertainment and distraction and toward fresh knowledge about yourself and your life. You might find additional fulfillment and meaning here. In any case, it's a way to meet new people.

3. Feel and Be Grateful

No matter what kind of major goal you are working toward, if you look around you will discover that it's already in your life on a smaller scale. You can feel it already, so set your magnet to attract it. Experience a sense of gratitude for what you already have, and your magnet will start working differently right away.

Timing *Is* Important

It has been shown that the effectiveness of an idea—even when developed by creative professionals—decreases to a mere 5 percent of its original energy within twelve days if it is not put into action. After two weeks, its power is almost completely gone. Intelligent managers know this, and they keep the flame burning by transforming initial enthusiasm into concrete action immediately.

You can use this information too, by following up on a good idea with immediate action. The first step might be to write down what you are excited about right now and lay out a rough plan for what you might do.

"What you tell me, I will forget. What you show me, I will remember. What you let me do, I will understand."

Confucius
Founder of Confucianism
551–479 BC

Online Dating: An Excursion into the Virtual World

Many people search online for the right partner. It seems to be a good approach, due to the large selection and relative ease of initiating contact with potential mates. Simultaneously, though, many people find that it doesn't really work, even after trying for a long time. If you apply your knowledge of the power of your magnetic heart, you will be able to understand the underlying reasons for this and become more effective in your search.

Seekers Find Rough Sailing on the Ocean of Relationships

◆ Most of the people who join an online dating site are "seeking." Even if that's not the main feeling you are experiencing, you are joining a large group whose magnets are projecting absence, disappointment, pain, emotional confusion, and other similar feelings. Unless you have truly outstanding abilities when it comes to emotional stability and setting limits, your own magnet will respond to this. And if you consciously set yourself apart from the group, you will not truly be able to connect with another person. Many have already recognized this dilemma, so they say they aren't searching for a partner—they just want to "meet new people."

◆ "Bad experiences" create an especially strong program for your magnet. This basic attitude forces a potential partner to jump over large hurdles and break through a protective barrier of mistrust before he or she can establish deep, human connection.

◆ People tend to seek partners using their logical brains, using parameters that the mind can understand—such as age, height, profession, astrological sign, nationality, etc. Anyone who has truly experienced love and intimacy will know that the most important "criteria" have nothing to do with logic.

◆ The sheer volume of potential partners is nearly impossible to sort through. Most relationship seekers have an ideal image in their heads, and anyone who fails to match this outward image doesn't make the first cut. Even an unflattering picture can be a roadblock.

◆ Many people aren't really looking for a partner or a romantic relationship. They're playing communication games.

◆ Our ideal image is often shaped by unrealistic expectations (based on films, for instance). That makes gritty, real relationships difficult.

◆ Searching for a partner online and still not finding someone when the options seem endless, only reinforces the sense that something is lacking in your life. After a few or several failed attempts, you may feel a growing sense of inadequacy or rejection, which can carry over into and affect your magnet.

Ivy and Gold Chains

Ivy, a divorced mother of two, had gone through a painful separation two years earlier. She had been married to a wealthy man for ten years, and the family had enjoyed a high standard of living. Ivy very much wanted to provide herself and her children with a similar lifestyle again.

Because of her former unhappy relationship, Ivy's first priority was to find a man who appreciated her, respected her as a valuable human being, and who also had "a certain status," as she put it.

After a long period of being single, she gathered her courage and decided to venture back into the dating world. She placed an ad and two pictures of herself on an online dating site. A very attractive woman, Ivy's inbox was soon flooded with responses.

After several unsatisfactory dates, she decided to make a correction. In her experience, there were certain characteristics that made men particularly undesirable. She decided to express this in her ad: "Men with gold chains and chest hair, please look elsewhere. I'm a woman with style."

She thought of a friend she liked very much who drove a nice sports car, and added, "If you drive a Porsche, for instance, that would be more my type."

Because of her unhappy marriage, Ivy really longed for a fulfilling physical relationship, which she saw as a symbol of appreciation and love—something that she hadn't received in the past few years. So she also included a short sentence about that.

Almost all of the men who responded after her revisions had chest hair or wore gold chains around their necks or wrists! Without exception, they were looking for a fling rather than a partnership. And none of them had a Porsche.

Ivy was completely mystified as to why her ad was attracting the exact men that she didn't want—especially since she had spelled out what she didn't like.

After learning about the secret of the mirror, she realized the reason: First of all, her magnetic heart was reliably attracting exactly what she had rejected. Secondly, while she was trying to avoid the superficial friendships and acquaintances from her past few years, she was also trying to join a group of people who displayed their wealth outwardly—which was still clearly reflected in her magnet.

Seven weeks after she discovered this, she met a single father while walking her children to school, and they fell in love. For the first time in twelve years, she felt that a man understood the core of her being and loved her for it.

Taking the Best Possible Advantage of Dating Sites

If you want to use dating sites for getting to know people, the following suggestions may help:

- Your clarity and your feelings are your magnet. Feel what you really want. Avoid expectations that no one person will be able to fulfill.
- Don't write down your demands. Write down what you have to offer. If you require too much, the other person will sense the experiences in your past that are causing neediness, which will then invite similar situations into your life.
- Spend less time describing what you do and more time saying how you feel when you do something.
- Don't say what you think you are. Let the readers decide that for themselves based upon what you write and how you write it. If you want to project that you're a sensitive person, don't say, "I'm sensitive." When you let others sense it through your writing style, you're letting your magnet do its work. For instance, you could describe a positive feeling that you have in certain situations, or quote part of a poem.
- Don't write anything concerning feelings springing from bad experiences. You will just attract more of them.
- Don't write anything about sex unless that's the main thing you are looking for. Positive, fulfilling physical intimacy will happen on its own when you find the right person. Write about love. True love makes beautiful sex happen by itself.
- Don't describe the situations or kinds of people you want to avoid, unless you want to magically attract just that.

◆ Don't string anyone along for tactical reasons unless you want to set your magnet to repel compassionate people. Someone who can sense your feelings in the way you want will realize what you're doing and won't play along.

◆ If you're hiding something important, you will attract people who are also hiding something significant.

◆ Try not to act counter to your true feelings, even if it's tempting. The more you do that, the more you damage your emotional magnet. Don't play with other people's emotions unless you want to attract people who will play with yours. Don't behave in a certain way simply to prove something to yourself.

◆ Don't hide your appearance. If you do, your magnet will project a weak sense of love for yourself. You will be much more attractive to people than you imagine as soon as you start liking what you see in the mirror. Invest in several nice, current pictures of yourself that make you happy whenever you look at them. Even if you're not planning to use them for a dating site, it's like giving yourself a bouquet of flowers. Set them up on your nightstand and/or post them online. That's your magnet.

◆ Don't use job application photos, and definitely avoid pictures with other people—like ex-partners—in them, even if they've been retouched or cut out. Look for a photographer who can really capture your feelings and tell him how you want to come across. A picture is a strong magnet, and everything in it has an effect.

◆ Forget about Hollywood unless you want to attract actors. If you're looking for people with a heart, project that you are also a person with a heart.

- If you want to attract someone who is admired and respected by other people, make sure your own writing radiates this.
- When you are chatting with, e-mailing, or meeting someone, try to sense what the other person is truly like. They are not fairytale princes or goddesses; they are human beings.
- Ask questions that involve the heart! What does he dream of? What moves him? What touches her heart? What hurts her? What does he fight for? When does he feel weak? What does she think about other people? How does she see her life and where she stands right now? Try to get a sense of whether he or she is a victim, and if so, how? How does he deal with his past? This will help you more quickly ascertain who the person really is on an authentic level, and it reduces your risk of falling prey to your own illusions.
- Don't be secretive about yourself unless you want your magnet to project a sense of distance. You are most attractive to other people when you let your heart guide you.

Resetting Your Magnet: The Disappearing Act

If you have been signed up with a dating service for a while and you haven't had any success yet, try the following experiment: Delete your profile. Don't just stop using it—discard it entirely, even if it was a lot of work putting it together. It's no loss really, because it obviously hasn't been helping you. The profile is old. It projects what you were like months or years ago, so it will keep attracting the same familiar types. Choose a time period when you will stop looking. It might be for three weeks or three months. Whatever feels right is the perfect decision.

Pay close attention to what you feel when you totally scratch your profile. You may experience more clarity after you do this. Often it feels like being freed from an obligation. This new sensation will change your magnet right away. Observe how your perceptions of people in your everyday life are altered. Feel your magnet start to radiate again.

Then, if you want, create a new profile after a waiting period. It will probably have different results than before. Or you may not feel like participating anymore. It's your own personal experiment.

If you find that others seem only superficially interested in you and appear to want something from you, look at yourself—are you truly interested in the other person's essence? In his or her hopes, fears, and uncertainties? Do you want to support this individual in these, or are you mainly trying to get something for yourself? Are you chasing a dream, or do you want to experience a real person?

 **Emotional Exercise: Sensing the Essence of Another Person**
Look the other person in the eyes, maybe while he or she is telling you something that is less interesting to you. As you do so, think to yourself, "I want to see the love in you." Try to see what's behind the person's eyes. Feel your own emotions.

When you meet a person and start to consider a long-term relationship, don't just pay attention to what you feel—also look at what "happens" in your encounters with one another.

Does love happen? Does joy happen?
Does gratitude happen? Does beauty happen?

In this case, beauty means the beauty of your mutual interactions, not external beauty.

173

Decisive Action: Reason and Purpose

Reason

◈ Your actions are a sign, especially for you. They create a feeling of clarity and strength within you, which gets projected outwardly.

◈ Your magnet brings people to your home. You open the door through your own action. When it comes to the power of your magnet, it's *not* important to do what will definitively bring you success later on, what's important is to do something—anything—about the issue in question.

◈ Action changes your projection in a specific area from "victim" to "creator." It allows you to break free from your rigid boundaries and sets a veritable river in motion.

Purpose

◈ The purpose of decisive action is to feel your own power, and thereby understand yourself. You will love yourself more for what you do and are, rather than criticizing yourself for what you're afraid to do.

Putting the Ninth Secret into Action

◆ Whenever you want to achieve something, put your heart into your action. Imagine that you can direct your magnet's projection toward places where it will work on its own for your benefit. Then, just wait and watch what happens.

◆ Do you know people who are "doers"? What do they have in common? They create success where others ruminate, hesitate, and accept failure fairly easily. Their "wins" more than make up for their "losses." Lack of success is not seen as a mistake but as a valuable lesson. What impression do these empowered people make on you? Do you see something in them that you would like to feel or project, too?

◆ Remember situations in which important events and people came to you like gifts. You made a decision…what was it? And you took action. But it wasn't the action itself that created your success—the result came to you through a completely different channel.

◆ If you wished for something for a long time and didn't get it, were you really acting decisively? Or were you responding like a victim, defending yourself in order to keep from being hurt again? Feel the difference between these two attitudes.

175

How to Reset Your Magnet

- As soon as you have developed an idea and made a decision, put it down in writing and develop a rough action plan. It doesn't need to be the "right" plan, but it should be a basic concept about how to act on the new plan. For your magnet to work, it's important to simply get the potential action in writing, transferring the (virtual) idea onto the (real) page.
- Take at least the first small step of this plan right away, or the next day.
- If you can, do something related to the plan every day, regardless of how small or large a step it is. This could even mean working on the plan itself.
- When you learn something new, correct your plan immediately so that you always feel like you're doing the best possible thing. Be "consistently flexible."
- Think hard about whether you will tell people about it, and if so, who you will tell. Sometimes another person's thoughtless comment is enough to discourage you. Having a little "secret" can sometimes create big miracles!

The Tenth Secret

"The most important time
in your life is now!
Everything that you feel
and think right now is
creating your future."

The Power of the Present

As you come to understand the effects of your magnet, you might long for a direct path toward cleaning out the old and creating something new. This path exists, and it will reveal itself to you if you integrate the power of the present into your life.

The more you live in the past, or feel the weight of your past as a burden, the more you will be immersed in old feelings. That creates a force of attraction in your magnet that draws people who want to experience these old emotions with you. You will keep living out your past in the present and future. In the affected area of your life, you may feel like a hamster running on a wheel. You can move as quickly or slowly as you want...but you're always on the same wheel.

There is a way to break free from this cycle and create a future that is truly new—a future that doesn't grow out of your past and is free from the burdens of old wounds.

Feel more and more of your life in the here and now! Make decisions and take action based on the present moment.

To do this, you will need to trust your life's path, and you will need another way to make decisions, other than constantly consulting your past for reference. You can find both of these things by inviting a different approach into your life—one that you may not be using very much right now.

The Cycle of Your Life in the Here And Now: Deciding, Acting, Accepting

Deciding in the Here and Now: Use the Strength of Your Intuition

Your Logical Mind: A Good Analyst, Planner, and Implementer
In day-to-day life, what may seem to be rational decisions are usually based on emotions. First, the logical mind considers the issue. It weighs experiences by remembering what it has heard, read, learned, and experienced. That's not really "rational"; it's emotional, because each of these experiences and internal films creates feelings. They are the ones that say to you: "Good or bad?" "Joy or fear?" and "Heaviness or lightness?"

Can you see the problem with this? It is slow and incomplete! The logical mind laboriously tells you a story. An emotion develops from the storyline, and you decide "yes," "no," or "maybe." Then another argument comes along, and you make another decision. If you're lucky, there will be plenty of yeses so that you can stop thinking about it and just make a decision. But you might also end up with a messy pile of yeses, no's, and maybes that are supposed to help you decide what to do. The result is a tangled pile of feelings, and often you are so uncertain that you don't act at all.

Additionally, your logical mind has a very limited repertoire of real facts, and they all come from your past. In other words, most of the information is out of date.

*Whenever your logical mind makes a decision,
the past is making the decision. It takes a little
bit of courage—the courage to do something
uncertain in the midst of such a decision—
to be rewarded with a new experience.*

Your Intuition: A Superior Decision-Maker

It's estimated that our conscious minds process about fifty basic informational units (bits) per second. That's relatively slow, and the volume of information is fairly small, so that you can call the result "thinking" and use words to explain it.

The subconscious, on the other hand, deals with several million bits per second. In the time that your logical mind takes to count to ten, your intuition has counted to well over five hundred thousand. Just as you're starting to consciously think about a problem, your intuition has already found the solution and is trying hard to tell you about it. You might not be able to hear it, though, because your conscious mind is still counting to ten and failing to come up with a solution. Instead of listening to your intuition, it starts counting from the beginning again because it suspects it may have missed a number.

Feelings Are the Language of Your Intuition

The results of any intuitive process are so well integrated, multilayered, and deep seated that you cannot comprehend them with your limited logical awareness. That's why the answer is given to you in the form of a feeling or sense. Some people call it a "gut feeling,"

180

while others call it "inner guidance," or simply "intuition." No matter what we call it, it's always the same skill.

As long as you are thinking hard about an issue, you're distracted and can't receive this emotional message. That's why many "enlightening" experiences come only after you stop trying to figure out the problem—like when a solution seems to magically pop into your head while you are showering.

You already have the enormous gift of intuitive skill. You don't need to do anything to help it along. All you need to do is start listening to it, and that is easy, too: Ask yourself questions, listen to yourself, try something out and feel if it is right. It's like learning a language. The more you practice, the more clearly and easily you will understand what is being said, and your confidence in this ability will grow.

"The intuitive spirit is a sacred gift and the rational spirit is a faithful servant. We have created a society that honors the servant and forgets about the gift."

Albert Einstein
Physicist and philosopher
1879–1955

A Brief Guide to Your Intuition

Over time, you will get to know your own intuition so well that you will not need an interpreter. You will simply be able to tell how you feel, and you won't act against it anymore. If you want to "awaken" your intuition to advise you on an issue, the following simple questions can help:

Does it feel "good" or "right"?
If not, what would feel good or right?

Don't search your mind for explanations. Just trust how you feel! It's enough to know whether something feels good or not. If you don't know how to sense this, see what it feels like when you think about various alternatives. You could start to follow one path and pay attention to how it makes you feel. Or you could go to a place (a new apartment, a new city, or a potential new office) and see how that makes you feel. If you don't sense a clear response—or you're still uncertain—ask more specific questions to get a "yes" or "no" answer.

An Intuitive "No" or "Bad" (Not in the Flow)
- Something's not right here!
- Something feels complicated or heavy (like a burden).
- I sense some inexplicable or invisible resistance, as though someone were putting on the brakes.
- I want to get out of here. I don't like it.
- External resistance and problems keep coming up.

An Intuitive "Yes" or "Good" (in the Flow)

◆ I feel lightness and joy when I think or do that.

◆ It feels easy.

◆ It feels like someone's "helping" me.

◆ I want to go here. I like it.

◆ New external doors keep opening up, almost like a miracle.

This survey is very helpful for your interactions with people. Evaluate how you feel as a relationship develops.

If you can't see a clear direction or response, it may be that you're not supposed to do anything at all right now. Ask yourself: "Do I really need to make a decision right now? What would it feel like if I decided to put everything on hold until some clear feelings surfaced?" That might be what it takes for your clarity to develop.

Acting in the Here and Now: Do What You Want to Experience, As Soon As Possible

If at all possible, don't put your life on hold for an uncertain future. That's often an escape mechanism. Feelings want to be experienced right now. They're like children: If you put them off too frequently, they become very unhappy, or the window of opportunity simply passes.

The Failed Life Bargain

Michael and Ashley met when they were economics students in college in their early twenties. They instantly fell in love, as if struck by lightning. Even years later, they were still sure they would spend their lives together. The couple felt such deep love for each other, along with a desire for freedom and adventure, that they made the following bargain: They would both use their educations to establish solid careers. Until they turned forty, they would spend all of their time and energy earning and saving as much money as possible. They would then use their "nest egg" to live together for the rest of their lives, fancy free. The duo worked hard, didn't buy much, and their assets grew as planned. At the age of thirty-eight, Ashley was killed in a car accident. Sadly, the lovers never got a chance to pursue their dream.

Fulfill your desired feelings as soon as you can. Of course you can still have goals, make plans, and follow your dreams. You can expand your skills and knowledge, and express yourself. But don't do it at the expense of the present moment. Other than change, the "here and now" is the only thing you can be sure of.

If You're Wondering Why Something Happened...

Maybe you have already seen for yourself that it's not a good idea to put off your happiness for the future. Suddenly, the beloved person who was part of your plans is gone. You both meant well, and now you're asking yourself how it could have happened.

Maybe it happened because you were both looking for love in the future, without recognizing that love can only exist right now. As a result, love was impossible to find. One or both of you had certain illusions. Maybe you believed that you could find better feelings somewhere else, with another person or at another time. More love. More fulfillment. More security. As a result, you put off what you could have been experiencing in that moment of being together.

No matter where you are in your relationship with someone, there's always room for more love and new, more intense experiences—as many as you want. The relationship can always grow deeper with this one particular person at your side. There's only one requirement: You both need to be aware of it, and you both need to want it.

If your partner isn't open to this, don't wait for him or her! If you stall, you will feel empty and closed off, and your magnet will project a sense of emptiness and being shut down.

We don't live to produce results, but to feel experiences.

Every change requires someone to take the first step, and sometimes even the second and third ones. It's not a problem, as long as you know that every step you take benefits you. You are doing it for yourself so that you can be free. Open yourself up to the feeling of loving your own life. You don't need a partner for this. Stay true to yourself and do what you expect the other person to do for you. Sometimes this can create a miracle.

*"Past love is only a memory. Future love is a dream and a wish. Only in the here and now can we truly love."**

Mahatma Gandhi
Pacifist and human rights activist
1869–1948

* This quote is also attributed to Gautama Buddha and other Buddhist teachers.

Healing Love: See What's Really There

Once you have decided not to hurt yourself anymore by closing off your heart, you will no longer be waiting for someone to come and "win" it, to storm the castle, as it were. Whatever feelings you put into your magnet will be attracted to you, too. If you expect someone to open your heart, someone will come along who is waiting for you to open his or her heart, too. And nothing will happen, or else someone will come along who will toy around with your heart in order to open it—and that doesn't feel good.

Instead, open it yourself. The more you want to understand the essence of other people, the more others will come along who also want to understand you as a person.

When you find someone, you have two choices: You can try to understand the surface of the encounter. You can listen to their stories, observe their behavior, and see what happens when you're together in order to compare all of this with your own ideas. You think about what the other person could give you. Alternatively, you can evaluate what's happening inside of you: How do you feel? How do you think the other person feels? Is there uncertainty or fear? Do you feel the same thing in yourself? You have been drawn to one another so that you can understand each other.

Wanting to know the future is a bit like sitting on a park bench on a warm spring day, enjoying an ice cream cone, and asking yourself, "What is the meaning of life?" It's absurd because you aren't living in the present moment.

Trust Your Life

It's true—whenever you open your heart, you always seem to get hurt. Again and again, you haven't gotten what you expected, and it was painful. You gave a great deal—all of your love—and instead of being rewarded, you were rejected. It's almost like the universe is trying to punish you for feeling love.

You might think you have only two options left: Closing yourself off so that you can't be hurt again; or taking a risk by opening yourself up to the danger of being hurt again. Maybe you have already tried a combination of opening and protecting yourself, and you have found that it's not a good way to find truly fulfilling love.

It's a seemingly impossible dilemma. Maybe you've decided not to worry about it anymore and to focus on your good friendships and work. Maybe you've even decided that no one person exists who can help you experience the depth and variety that you dream of—or that you've already experienced the best you ever will.

However you choose to explain this to yourself, something deep inside you may feel incredibly sad and unfulfilled.

The Here and Now As a Way to Feel More Love

The conflict you feel between opening yourself up and protecting yourself is nothing more than the history (a story) of your thoughts based upon past experiences. As long as you think in terms of opening versus protecting, it is impossible to find a solution—your thoughts themselves are the problem.

You can test this for yourself. Imagine someone with whom you would like to be more open or someone you want to protect yourself from. Then, try a simple thought experiment: Imagine what it would feel like if you knew for sure that hearts aren't capable of opening or closing. Let's assume for a minute that this is true. What would it feel like? Try it, and see. Do you feel relief? Less pressure? This might help you to accept the heart as it is—susceptible to outside influences.

The inner peace, joy, or relief that you might be feeling right now comes from the fact that you are completely in the present. You no longer have concerns about opening or closing the heart. You have calmed the painful storm of your thoughts. If you met another person while you were in this state, he or she would see you as being "centered" or "grounded." And you would see the other exactly as he or she is in that moment.

Solutions for Your Heart and Love

◆ Decide not to be a victim of your past anymore.

◆ Decide that you don't want to know what another person can do for you, but that you want to feel what happens when you are with them.

◆ Don't search for a "partner" or some other kind of emotional provider; instead, enjoy the experience of perceiving people the way they truly are. Take an interest in what they love, how they feel in the moment, what they long for, and what ideas they have about the future.

◆ Talk less about the past, especially when it involves painful relationships. Your conversation partner has experienced the same thing, and when you focus on it, you both activate your old emotional patterns and transfer them to your magnets.

◆ Compare less; observe more.

◆ Allow yourself to have "no opinion" about things, but remain interested in other people's opinions. The reason why someone has an opinion is often more interesting than the opinion itself.

◆ Allow yourself to know nothing about certain topics. Notice how nice and freeing it feels.

When we see each other first and foremost as human beings, and only afterward as men and women with certain roles to play, our hearts can begin to communicate. Only then will we think less about what someone else can give us, and sense more who that other person is and what is happening between us in a particular moment. We will also become more aware of ourselves, of our own feelings, as well as how we are feeling about the other person. Through this, we receive the greatest gift of all: Love for what is happening in the present.

Start by trying not to take your past so seriously anymore. The more you notice where you are in the now—what you are feeling, whom you are with, and what you are experiencing—the more you will realize that your past isn't really that important. What you are experiencing now is the only thing that you have.

The more you realize this, the more courage you will have to let love develop within you.

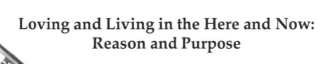

Loving and Living in the Here and Now: Reason and Purpose

Reason

- Love can only be felt in the here and now. You can't remember love. You can only have memories that cause you to feel love now. You can recognize this because the feeling of love fades when the memory disappears.
- Feelings cannot be put off for the future. Has that ever worked? Hoping for more happiness in the future distracts you from opportunities to feel love now.
- Your aura is made up of your feelings. If you put off positive feelings for some time in the future, you will have a lack of positive feelings now. What will this absence draw to you?

Purpose

- The purpose of realizing that love has no past and no future is being able to feel yourself in the here and now—and accepting how you are and what is happening. The more you can love and enjoy what you have now—because that's the only thing you truly have—the more happiness you will feel and radiate.

Putting the Tenth Secret into Practice

◆ In the book of your life, can you remember chapters when you were waiting for a better future in a relationship? How often did it work? How often did things turn out differently than you had hoped?

◆ Observe people who are always making plans and hoping for—or working toward—a supposedly better future. How do these people seem to you? Do they create a good feeling within you? Do you want to be like them?

◆ When you watch someone who is completely absorbed in a creative activity, like painting a picture or making music, how does it make you feel? Can you feel how just watching a person living fully in the moment affects your mood? That's how you will affect other people the more you learn to love every moment of your life.

How to Reset Your Magnet

◆ When you hold on to unpleasant memories, you create feelings that no longer have any basis in the here and now. You program your magnet to attract more people and events that produce similar feelings.

◆ A better approach: Find the positive aspects of a past situation. There's always something. For instance, you may have grown because of a situation that you overcame. Without these experiences, you wouldn't be the person you are today.

◆ When you hang on to unpleasant memories and think about what you have lost, you transfer feelings of loss to your magnet now.

◆ A better approach: You can see the glass of your life as half full or half empty. Exercise the half-full perspective and discover the gifts in your life right now.

◆ Do you have an internal "shrine" that is preserving remnants from your past or a specific person from an old relationship? It will block new things from happening in this area. Take the shrine apart and choose your current life instead—which begins anew with every moment.

◆ Go ahead and consult your logical mind, but try listening to your intuition more frequently. That's how you will find it: your very own path to a life that is fulfilled in every way.

"May your heart magnet guide you through your life journey and to your deepest fulfillment!"

What the Mirror Reveals

Issues	Possible Causes in My Magnet
Observe: What do I notice about myself?	*Understand: What is my "internal film," my expectations?*
I attract "unavailable" partners, or partners with a fear of commitment. I'm afraid of too much commitment myself, though I long for intimacy.	• I'm afraid of losing my freedom in a relationship. I don't want anyone to "own" me. I'm afraid of losing myself in the other person. • I have an incorrect understanding of what freedom really means. • I'm afraid of not being able to fulfill the requirements of a romantic relationship. • A partner who is afraid of commitment doesn't pose any "risk" [to me] that one day a commitment will suddenly be required. • I actually love the adventure of new relationships more than being in a stable long-term relationship.
I attract partners with a fear of commitment even though I love intense connections more than anything and have experienced them in the past.	• My fear of loss attracts partners with a fear of commitment (one cause of this is fear of loss). I am desperate to forge an intense bond very quickly because I feel it will protect me from loneliness and my fear of being abandoned.
I attract people who are dishonest with me.	• I strongly reject dishonesty because…(my parents, my ex-partner were dishonest…) • I have found that I tend to be inauthentic in certain situations. That disturbs me about myself, so it particularly disturbs me in other people (thus attracting them).
I attract people who don't know what they want and/or can't make decisions or won't make a commitment to me.	• I am uncertain or lack clarity about what I want or what might happen if I made a clear decision. • I am afraid of being rejected or punished by love being withheld if I am myself. • I don't really make a decision about the other person—I wait for him/her to commit to me first.
I attract people who lie about their feelings.	• I sometimes lie to myself about my own feelings because I have such a strong desire to experience these feelings. • I lie to others about my feelings in the hope that they will give me certain feelings in return.
My life mainly consists of a series of problems.	• I have the idea that I am a complicated person. • I have an attitude that other people need to learn how to deal with me. • I am convinced that I have problems other people don't have. • I am convinced that life is made up of challenges to be solved. • I am convinced that there is good and bad luck.

Pathways to Resolution and a New Direction
Make a change: What is my new decision?

- I can recognize that as long as I am trying to hold onto my freedom and prove that I have it, I am not free; I am a slave to my idea of freedom.
- I can recognize that no one can give or take away my freedom. Freedom exists as soon as I recognize that I am always the one making the decision.
- I can recognize that true love feels like freedom and deep understanding.
- I can recognize that true freedom means completely committing myself, without feeling a mountain of obligation.
- I can recognize that if the other person seems to be "demanding" something from me, he or she is actually telling me their own narrative about intimacy and relationships. It's not a restriction, it's just a story—and it's up to me whether I like and agree with it or not.

- I can give myself permission to be afraid of loss. It's a fundamental human fear, and it's normal.
- I can recognize that we all constantly have to decide whether we will close ourselves off to love or whether we will have the courage to keep opening ourselves up, because life without intimacy and love is meaningless.

- I can recognize that "absolute truth" is an illusion. There are only perspectives, and everyone's perspective is different.
- People are who they are, and they do what they do. No one is honest all the time. Who am I to tell someone else how he or she should be?
- I can recognize that to some extent, everyone carries every kind of disposition within themselves— even me. I am allowed to be anything I want: Loving or angry, fair or unfair, honest or dishonest, brave or fearful.... It's part of being human, and it is not a flaw.

- Decide, decide, decide! Never "against" something—always "in favor of" something. In particular, decide in favor of a person, of love, of feelings, of joy, of my own life values. And observe. Keep noticing that everything is the result of my own decisions, whether conscious or unconscious. I will feel a sense of clarity, which will attract other people who have clarity, or will inspire them to become clearer themselves.

- Closely observe how people lie to themselves. Don't judge them but rather try to sense what they are really like beyond how they are acting. Try to understand why they are doing this. What are they afraid of? What are they really looking for? Knowing that will help me understand more about myself, too.

- Know that each of these convictions is the *cause* of an attraction in my magnet, not the result. As long as I believe in something, it will continue to be true.
- Understand that each of these convictions is just a story created by my thoughts. Almost none of them are true if I look at them more closely. Where do they come from (parents, partners, ...)?
- Move away from "problems" and toward "events," which are made up of cause and effect.
- I can recognize that past events are only memories. I can keep thinking about them, or I can leave them alone and think about my life "from now on." Each moment is a new start for my life.

(cont'd.)

What the Mirror Reveals (cont'd.)

Issues	Possible Causes in My Magnet
Observe: What do I notice about myself?	*Understand: What is my "internal film," my expectations?*
My relationships are usually very intense, often dramatic or complicated, but end up being unfulfilling for me.	• I am convinced that love and dramatic feelings belong together. • I am convinced that harmony would be boring. • I have the idea that butterflies (fear) have something to do with love, and their absence indicates too little love.
My life and/or my relationships are characterized by "chaos."	• I have no inner clarity, and take no decisions, no decisive action. • I have no sense of why I am here and what specifically I want to experience. • I am not really free. I may still be hung up on memories of a past relationship.
I attract people who have very specific behaviors that tell me they don't respect me. *I attract people who gradually exhibit more and more behaviors that I dislike.*	• I have turned an observed behavior into an important personal symbol of rejection (that is my internal film). • I judge people harshly according to certain behaviors, and I develop a sense of rejection or agreement based on this. I often "condemn" people.
I love "strong" personalities and attract them, and then I am treated disrespectfully. *I attract people who want to exhibit power or violence toward me.*	• I admire people who can do more or have achieved more than I can do/have done. • I strongly dislike something about myself (e.g., my body). • Under no circumstances do I want another uncharismatic, powerless partner.
I want to attract especially masculine/feminine partners, but I always find the opposite.	• I find myself not feminine or masculine enough.
I want to attract especially masculine/feminine partners, and I do, but they quickly leave.	• After I get a certain level of affection from the other person, I start doubting it. I question whether he or she is really sincere in their affection for me, or is being honest with me (a self-esteem issue). • After reaching a certain level of intimacy/being in love, I set my partner up as "something very special" and feel inferior to him or her (also a self-esteem issue).

Pathwaysto Resolution and a New Direction

Make a change: What is my new decision?

- I can write down my own convictions (!) and review them: Are they really true?
- I can write down my own goals: What do I really want? What qualities should a functional relationship have? What does it take for me to view a relationship positively and be prepared to fill it with life? Even later on, after several months and on a daily basis? What am I prepared to change in my life in order to make a functional partnership possible?
- I can ask myself, "Am I ready to grow with another person and to share my time and space?"

- I can clean up! I can make decisions in every area of my life, including outside the relationship. How does my apartment look? My car? The contents of my basement? My closet? My workplace? Am I managing chaos or shaping my own life?
- I can gain clarity: Do I really know what I want? I can write it down. Some visions might sound nice, but they are practically impossible to implement because they contradict each other. I can discover whether the idea is really feasible: Are there contradictions? If so, I can make a new decision!
- I can assess my "inner room." Is it there? Is it free?

- Let me evaluate: Is it true that this behavior always represents what I think it does? What else could it mean from another person's perspective? Assuming that the other person does in fact respect me, why does he or she keep doing what he or she is doing?
- I can go on an imaginary journey: What would it be like if a person who obviously loves me deeply unconsciously exhibits this behavior? Would it be bad? Or could I learn to love it because I love the person?

- I can recognize that no one in the world is better or worse than I am. Some people have certain characteristics that complement or challenge me, or qualities that can teach me something.
- I can write down and put together a list of why/where/when am I, or was I, a strong person.
- I can gain clarity! What are my apparent weaknesses and what do I think about them? What do I dislike about myself? Why? Is it even true? Assuming that I am perfect just the way I am, couldn't those same characteristics be seen as strengths?
- I can think about why I admire powerful or "strong" people? How do I feel when I'm with these people?

- I could use the "internal switch" to change what I am projecting. I don't need to change my behavior—just to observe the effects of the switch.

- I can feel more love for my own life.
- I can remember and sense the life feeling I chose for myself, and feel—regardless of other people— how my life is on the right track to get me there.
- I can use my "internal switch" to change what I am projecting. I needn't change my behavior—I can just observe the effects of the switch.

About the Author

Ruediger Schache is a consciousness researcher, author, freelance journalist, seminar leader, coach and speaker. After completing his degree in business and psychology, he spent many years as a manager at a successful industrial company before becoming a journalist and author.

During countless trips through the United States, Mexico and Asia, as well as two years at a therapeutic center in Brazil, he took many courses that led him to a deep, integrative understanding of the connections between personal reality, love, relationships and the meaning of human life. Today, through books, seminars, presentations and consulting sessions, he shares his deep understanding of these internal and external connections between life's key issues.

More about Ruediger Schache's work

Internationally renowned author Ruediger Schache's books have sold over 2 million copies worldwide and have been published in 26 languages. *Das Geheimnis des Herzmagneten* (the German edition of *Your Magnetic Heart*) was on the prestigious *Spiegel* bestseller list for 84 weeks.

Schache has been dedicated to writing and science from childhood on. Today, one of his outstanding skills is to build, in an engaging way, a bridge between scientific knowledge, spiritual truth and practical life. "Between spiritual awakening, ways to enlightenment and a scientific world view there is no incompatibility," says Schache. "There is only ignorance and knowledge. Questions and discoveries. Unconsciousness and consciousness. In the deepest truth, in relationships, in life or in the world, there are no right or wrong happenings. There is only what IS, and the forces that shape it. Understand these forces and you understand creation and its meaning. And then it all becomes quiet and calm within you."

In addition to his work as a speaker and author, Ruediger Schache and his wife, naturopath Nicole Diana Engelhardt, run the Institute for Consciousness Research and a surgery for New Medicine near Munich.

You can interact with Ruediger Schache and view more of his published work—nonfiction and fiction books, CDs, card decks and apps—at his website, www.ruedigerschache.com. Click on the U.K. flag to read the site in English.

Printed in the USA
CPSIA information can be obtained
at www.ICGtesting.com
JSHW022335140824
68134JS00019B/1491